AF574159

SOUTHERN ELECTRIC MULTIPLE-UNITS

1948-1983

S 8
S 10

SOUTHERN ELECTRIC MULTIPLE-UNITS

1948-1983

COLIN J. MARSDEN

LONDON
IAN ALLAN LTD

First published 1983

ISBN 0 7110 1314 4

Published by Ian Allan Ltd, Shepperton, Surrey; and printed by Ian Allan Printing Ltd at their works at Coombelands in Runnymede, England

Contents

Cover
The pioneer 4VEP Class 423 high-density outer suburban unit No 7701 departs from London Road station, Guildford, with an afternoon Guildford-Waterloo via Cobham service during 1982. *Andrew French*

Left
Throughout the 1970s and early 1980s the main stamping ground for CEP units (classified by BR as Class 411) has been the SED main line, with a handful of units operating on the CD and allocated to Brighton. Set No 7198 in Inter-City livery hurries with a Victoria-Gillingham train near Rochester on 20 March 1978. *Colin Marsden*

Introduction

Welcome to the second volume of *Southern Electric Multiple-Units*. The 35 years covered, 1948-1983, have probably seen the greatest changes in railway and stock operation this country has ever seen, with the elimination of steam traction throughout the country and the virtual replacement of locomotive hauled trains on SR main and branch lines, with emus. The 1951 design EPB units are the earliest types covered in this volume and in real terms are only a technical update of the well established SUB design, dating back to the 1920s. As Southern Railway stock was up for replacement new sets were authorised, closely following the design of the SR stock it was to replace in terms of passenger accommodation, but mechanically and electrically greatly advanced.

Passenger accommodation slowly improved during the 1950s culminating in the redesignation on 3 June 1956 of third class accommodation to second. With the provision of modern mechanical cleaning aids trains were being kept in a cleaner condition, therefore providing a better travelling atmosphere for the passengers. During the late 1950s new stock was introduced for the various Kent Coast electrification programmes, with both main line and outer-suburban stock being built, replacement stock for the Brighton and Portsmouth lines was introduced during the 1960s and 1970s. One of the greatest steps forward in electric multiple-unit traction came in 1966/7 with the full electrification of the Waterloo-Bournemouth line and the design of a push-pull system for through services to Bournemouth and Weymouth.

Towards the end of the 1960s and BRB published plans for the modernisation of much of the local and commuter services in the country, and during 1970 prototype high-density stock with each axle powered was built for evaluation trials on SR. This eventually led to modern emus on four of the BR regions. In 1982 the next step forward in SR emu design was unveiled, when the first Class 455 unit was introduced to the region.

At the end of 1982 the SR had a fleet of 1,164 units formed of 4,198 coaches — operating over 80% of the SR's services. During the coming years new generation emu stock will emerge to replace many of the 1951 design units and before the end of the decade new stock will be built for the Bournemouth line. Refurbishment programmes on 1951/7 Class 415, 416 (EPB), 410 (4BEP) and 411 (4CEP) units are now well underway and when completed during the latter part of the decade will provide efficient emu power into the 21st century.

The study of the emu classes has always taken second place amongst enthusiasts, except for members of certain organisations who specialise in the field. It is hoped that in the coming years more attention will be devoted to the unit field and more enthusiasts will find interest in the subject.

I would like to record my thanks to Mr G. Smith of the BR Public Affairs Office, Waterloo for his valuable assistance in providing some of the older illustrations included in this project, to Mr J. N. Faulkner for his assistance with chronological information, to Mrs J. W. Marsden for typing manuscripts and captions, and to the many photographers who placed their collections at my disposal during the preparation of this book.

Colin Marsden
Surbiton
February 1983

Coach Classifications

Although in the write-ups on each type throughout this book reference is made to first and second class seating, prior to 1956 seating arrangement was first and third class.

DMS Driving Motor Second
DTC Driving Trailer Composite
DTS Driving Trailer Second

MBSO Motor Brake Second Open
MLV Motor Luggage Van
MS Motor Second
MSO Motor Second Open

RB Restaurant Buffet

TBC Trailer Brake Composite
TBS Trailer Brake Second
TCK Trailer Composite Corridor
TLV Trailer Luggage Van
TRB Trailer Restaurant Buffet
TS Trailer Second
TSO Trailer Second Open
TSK Trailer Second Corridor

EPB

During late 1951 the first of a new generation of emu started to emerge, although being a direct descendant of the 4SUB units, new, modern and novel ideas were incorporated. The major change in SR emus was the fitting of the electro-pneumatic (EP) brake in addition to a Westinghouse brake, and it is from this fitting that the units get their type code EPB (Electro Pneumatic Brake). Passenger accommodation was similar to the last of the SUB builds, and coach types were the same, ie: MBSO (Motor Brake Second Open), TS (Trailer Second), TS (Trailer Second), MBSO (Motor Brake Second Open), one TS of each train being a compartment car, while the other was an open. MBSO vehicles contain all traction equipment with two 250hp English Electric traction motors being carried on the leading bogies. Total passenger accommodation being, MBSO vehicles 82 in the 3+2 style, TS (open) 112 in 3+2 style, TS (compartment) 120 in 10 compartments of 12. Another change from previous Southern tradition was the fitting of buckeye couplings and rubbing plates on the unit ends, together with high level air and control jumpers. Power for control and lighting was fed from a 70v MG (motor generator) instead of at line voltage via a potentiometer as on the SUB stock. After the first unit emerged from Eastleigh works carrying running number 5001 at the end of 1951, testing was carried out at Wimbledon depot with trial running on the New Guildford line. When delivered this unit was allocated car numbers continuing on from the SUB numbering range, however these were altered to a new range of numbers prior to the unit commencing passenger operation. During early 1952 the second production unit No 5002 emerged and a further 13 units entered traffic before the end of the year. Further orders were placed and Eastleigh built more than 200 units, Nos 5016-5048 emerging during 1953, and 5049-5053 during 1954. Late in 1953 a separate fleet of units started to emerge from Eastleigh numbered in the 51xx range, these were identical to earlier sets but were mounted on central style bogies. As time proved, no further units of the earlier number range and fitted with the Eastern style bogies were built, and those already in traffic were subsequently re-bogied. The fleet continued in the 51xx/52xx range until 1957 when unit No 5260 emerged. Minor detail differences do exist between units of various years, but all sets conform to the same basic design. By 1957 units could be seen in operation on all three sections of SR providing the backbone of the modern sub-

1
After its delivery the prototype SR designed 4EPB was allocated to Wimbledon Park, for initial 'on road' testing. When delivered the unit carried coach numbers continuing on numerically in the 4SUB series, however these were altered to a new range during 1952. Carrying the S prefix to its running number, No 5001 stands at Wimbledon Park during November 1951. *British Railways*

urban system. The next construction of units under the SR EPB classification was a fleet of two-car units built on reclaimed SR NOL unit frames, these were built at Eastleigh during 1959. The MBSO vehicle was of identical construction to those built for four-car sets, while the DTS (Driving Trailer Second) had a small, driver's full width cab with access vestibule behind, passenger accommodation being provided in two open saloons, one with four and the other with five bays, total unit seating capacity being 178. Running numbers allocated were 5651-5684. When built units initially operated on the Waterloo-Windsor/Weybridge line, but in more recent years have been allocated to the Central Division at Selhurst for use on suburban services.

During the late 1950s plans were drawn up for further fleets of suburban units of the same style as the 1951 Southern designed EPB units, however to BR standard coach design. The first units of the BR EPB fleet emerged from Eastleigh works during 1960 and were four-car sets. Internally units were very similar in design to previous SR sets but the body profiles were of a more smooth appearance and the technical specification was altered. The initial order was for 56 units, numbered in the 53xx range, two of which, Nos 5301 and 5302, were to be formed using SR designed trailers, while the remainder would have all BR designed vehicles. The MBSO cars have standard driving cabs with a guard's van behind to give access to the cab. Passenger accommodation is in two four-bay saloons set out in a 3+2 configuration. Traction equipment is mounted on the leading bogie of both MBSO cars, as on the SR units. Between the power vehicles are two TS cars of similar build each having five compartments at one end, and a five bay saloon at the other. When units entered traffic they were allocated to the Central and South Eastern Divisions where they have remained until today. A further 14 units of identical construction, were built at Eastleigh during 1962/3, for use on the South Western Division, however these did not operate on their intended division for many years and were soon to be seen operating with their elder sisters on the Central and Eastern Divisions.

A fleet of 79 two-car EPB units built to the BR design was constructed at Eastleigh between 1954-1958 primarily for the South Eastern Division to enable the formation of 10-coach trains on selected suburban routes numbers allocated were in 57xx range. Although this batch of units was constructed to the BR standard design, the earlier 1951 type electro-contactor control equipment was fitted. MBSO vehicles were of identical design to those used on the BR designed four-car sets, while the DTS vehicles contained five compartments and a four bay saloon, giving a total capacity of 186. In 1954/55 a fleet of 15 two-car EPB units fitted with 1951 style equipment was built for the North Eastern Region, to work on the Newcastle and South Shields third-rail electric system. These units resembled the SR fleet of the period except that a larger luggage van was provided and thus the MBSO passenger accommodation was

2
From an early date one of the strongholds for the EPB type was on South Eastern Division lines, radiating from Charing Cross and Cannon Street to South East London and Kent. EPB No S5179 departs from Catford Bridge with a Charing Cross-Hayes service on 13 August 1960 and passes under the Nunhead-Shortlands line. *John Scrace*

reduced to two saloons, one having three and other four bays. As headcodes were not used on the North Eastern system the front end carried marker lights and a destination indicator. When the Newcastle system was de-electrified in 1963, the units were only eight years old and it was decided to convert and transfer them to SR operating requirements, ie: fitting of a headcode and removing the destination indicator, and renumbering in the 5781-95 range.

During 1964 when new power was required for the Reading-Tonbridge line six of the BR built 2EPBs Nos 5701/04/08-11 were disbanded and their DTS vehicles reformed with spare Hastings profile demu stock to make six 3R demus, the spare motor cars being placed into store. Following this many reforms of SR and BR units took place but in time most units reverted to their original form.

When built EPB units were painted in standard green livery, subsequently changing to all blue during the 1960s and from the early 1980s units of all types have emerged painted in blue/grey livery.

During 1976/7 four of the SR designed 2HAP(SAP) units were disbanded and their MBSO vehicles used to form two new 4EPB units, their trailer cars coming from spares, and being numbered 5263/4. Shortly after this set No 5263 was selected to undergo face-lifting, this as a prototype of what could be done to the entire fleet on a long term basis. The unit was shopped at Eastleigh and emerged with new lower ceilings, fluorescent lighting, and more modern decor including being painted in Inter-City livery. Once back in traffic the unit was displayed and accepted, and by 1979 a major facelifting programme was authorised, this work also including the converting of all trailer compartment vehicles to open standards and the fitting of public address equipment. The contract was divided between the BREL works at Eastleigh and Horwich where work commenced during 1980. Included in this programme were the majority of 56xx 2HAP(SAP) MBSO vehicles, being formed in pairs with 'spare' EPB trailers or converted SUB vehicles to EPB standards. All facelifted units were renumbered in the 54xx range and are currently allocated to Selhurst. During 1982 a further facelifting programme was authorised this time for the 56xx 2EPB units. Work has included the fitting of fluorescent lighting, new lower ceilings, fitting of a doorway between the two saloons in the MBSO vehicle, and public address equipment. Units so treated have been renumbered in the 63xx range.

From the end of 1982 Eastleigh works commenced a facelift programme of the BR designed four cars sets, this work has included the opening out of all vehicles to SO standards and generally updating the units in line with the 415/4s.

Under the BR numerical classification the following codes were given:

Original SR designed 4EPB units	415/1
BR designed 4EPB units	415/2
Facelifted SR designed 4EPB units	415/4
Facelifted BR designed 4EPB units	415/6
BR designed 2EPB units	416/2
Facelifted 2EPB units	416/3

3
Such was the success of the EPB design, that during the early 1950s BR placed orders for additional fleets of two and four-car units of a slightly modified (BR) design, the most noticeable difference being the slab sided and flatter front appearance. Two-car No 5772 leads a 10-car formation of EPB stock out of Cannon Street on 6 May 1957 with the 17.02 Dartford via Sidcup service. *Brian Morrison*

4
Portrait of a BR designed two-car unit from the driving trailer second end. When this photograph was taken on 3 June 1954 the unit was new and would have been painted in green livery with grey roof. The front end fittings are of a different appearance to that of today, with a whistle above the driver's window in place of the two tone roof mounted horns, power jumper on the front end, and large sized route indicator numerals. *British Railways*

5
Units that entered traffic before June 1956 were designated as third class, but from then onwards the third class label gave way to second class accommodation. Of the SR designed four-car units one of the trailers was of the compartment type whilst the other was of an open layout; this view shows the interior of the third class open trailer from unit No S5001. It will be noticed that seating was laid out in the high density mode (3+2) with strung luggage racks overhead. *British Railways*

6
In 1954/5 Eastleigh works produced a fleet of 15 two-car (EPB) units for the North Eastern Region for use on the Newcastle electrification, as illustrated here. After de-electrification of the line in 1963 the units were converted for SR use and classified as 2EPB. The 16.03 Newcastle Central-South Shields awaits departure on 19 May 1982 with car No E65316 leading; this is now unit No 5786 on the SR. *M. Mensing*

7
A four-car formation of 'Tyneside' EPB stock stands at Hebburn with a stopping service from Newcastle to South Shields. It will be observed that when these units were in operation on the North Eastern, destination blinds and front/rear marker lights were used, in place of the conventional headcode unit. *P. J. Sharpe*

8
Over the years various liveries have adorned the EPB fleet and perhaps one of the most pleasing to the eye was green with full yellow warning ends, displayed here on SR unit No 5249 approaching Waterloo East with a Charing Cross-Dartford service on 18 June 1970. Roof mounted warning horns had by now been fitted. *A. W. Hobson*

STOPPING
E 65316

SOUTH SHIELDS
STOPPING

Continental
Corner Restaurant

5667
18

5106
58

17

9
The fleets of SR and BR designed two-car units have always been associated with branch line workings, quite often performing duties singly. SR designed 2EPB No 5667 stops at Datchet with the 13.38 Windsor & Eton Riverside-Waterloo service on 18 April 1966. The livery displayed is green with small yellow warning panel. *John Scrace*

10
EPB fleets operate today on all three divisions of the Region working on the suburban network. South Western allocated set No 5106 painted in standard rail blue livery departs from Twickenham with a Waterloo-Windsor & Eton Riverside train on 5 March 1980. *Colin Marsden*

11
Allocation of the fleet is currently divided between Wimbledon — WD (SWD), Selhurst — SU (CD) and Slade Green — SG (SED), however it is likely that with the introduction of new stock during the 1980s allocations will be amended. No 5111 passes through some lovely Surrey countryside near Epsom while forming the 15.42 Waterloo-Dorking service on 5 September 1981. *Colin Marsden*

12
This illustration serves as a useful comparison between the SR and BR builds; an SR built unit stands on the left with a BR designed set on the right. Differences will clearly be noted in the cab roof area, the arrangement of the roof mounted equipment and the visually flatter front of the BR unit. No 5048 forms the rear four coaches of a Dartford-Charing Cross service, while 2EPB No 5725 leads a Charing Cross-Dartford service at Slade Green on 6 February 1982. *Colin Marsden*

13
When viewing the BR designed four-car units from above, it will be observed that the coach roofs only carry ventilators, unlike the SR built units which have a mass of electric conduit. No 5304 passes Hither Green diesel depot on 3 July 1971 while working the 11.01 Sevenoaks-Charing Cross service. In the diesel depot stand three Class 08 shunting locomotives and a Class 33 diesel-electric. *D. A. Bosomworth*

14
Carrying the fast Waterloo-Bournemouth/Weymouth headcode, 2EPB No 5666 hurries through Deepcut between Brookwood and Farnborough on 15 April 1980 while working empty from Selhurst to Eastleigh Works for attention. The black triangle on the front indicates that the guard's compartment and traction equipment is at that end of the two-car unit. *Colin Marsden*

15
Two-car units are used in abundance on the South Eastern Division, however several sets are allocated to the SWD and CD, normally being used in twos or threes on suburban workings. Three two-car units depart from New Malden with a Waterloo (Windsor)-Waterloo (Main) service on 3 December 1979. (The second unit in the formation was formerly a NE 'Tyneside' set, recognisable by the larger brake van). *Colin Marsden*

16
During peak periods there are several Waterloo-Woking stopping services and during the early 1980s these were often formed of 2EPB formations. Departing from Surbiton and crossing from the up local to main line, an eight-car formation is led by unit No 5755 on 3 April 1980. *Colin Marsden*

17
After their re-allocation to the SR the former Tyneside units lost their destination indicators and marker lights in favour of a two position headcode system, in common with all other SR units, however inside the cabs the destination equipment is still partially intact. Set No 5791 eases its way round the tight curve into Weybridge while working a service from Staines on 28 March 1981. *Colin Marsden*

18
The fleet of units built for NE operation were fitted with a larger luggage van, than the similar sets used on SR and remained unaltered on reallocation to the SR, when a smaller than usual headcode box was fitted, giving enthusiasts another means of identification of the type. Set No 5782 leading a 4VEP passes Clapham Junction with a Waterloo-Portsmouth stopping service on 3 June 1981. *Colin Marsden*

WINTHROP
5755
10

5791

5782
73

19
The railway workshops at Eastleigh undertake all classified repairs to the SR emu fleet, except for extended maintenance such as facelifts or refurbishment which is undertaken at Swindon and Horwich. Whilst receiving a general overhaul at Eastleigh set No 5732 stands in the works yard minus much of its equipment and doors on 19 April 1979. *Colin Marsden*

20
As part of BR's efforts to improve the appearance of its rolling stock, from 1980 when units received repaints they were outshopped in blue/grey Inter-City livery, perhaps not giving the public a good foresight to Inter-City stock, but undoubtedly a vast improvement on the previous rather drab all blue. Resplendent unit No 5053 leads a not so clean sister near Crayford on 29 May 1981. *Colin Marsden*

21
The Elmers End to Hayes (Kent) branch has for many years been a stronghold for the EPB types. SR designed set No 5155 awaits departure for Charing Cross with the 13.55hrs service on 3 October 1982. This unit is allocated to Slade Green and the SG shed sticker can be seen behind the air pipes below the driver's window. *Michael Collins*

22
With Slade Green emu servicing depot in the background Class 415/2 (4EPB) No 5364 slows for the station stop with a Dartford-Charing Cross service on 6 February 1982. In common with SR designed units the majority of the BR built sets are now painted in blue-grey livery. This repaint is usually carried out at Selhurst between classified repairs.
Colin Marsden

23
In 1976 two SR designed 2HAP units were disbanded, giving their driving motor vehicles, basically identical to the SR EPBs, to a new 4EPB unit, with the trailer vehicles supplied from regional spares. When this unit, No 5263 took up operation in 1977 it was the first suburban unit to carry blue-grey livery on the SR. The set is seen here departing from Waterloo on a Chessington line service.
Colin Marsden

24
Once it was known that vast numbers of new units would not be made available to the SR for several years, an EPB facelift programme was put in hand during 1979. As Eastleigh would not be able to cope with the required output Horwich works was awarded part of the contract. Here the driving vehicle from unit No 5234 stands in the main erecting shop at Horwich on 3 October 1981 during facelift. *Colin Marsden*

25
One of the problems encountered with part of the facelift programme being carried out at Horwich Works near Bolton, is the transportation of stock to and from the SR. Normally units are made ready for transit at Selhurst and hauled by the SR to Willesden, from where the LMR take over; arrangements being reversed for the return journey. Whilst being returned to the SR set No 5424 became defective at Stockport and had to be recessed for repairs to be made. The unit is shown stabled in the station sidings on 27 December 1981. *John Chalcraft*

26
All units that have undergone facelift overhaul are renumbered into the six figure TOPS system, although only the last four digits are actually carried on the unit ends; all sets are allocated to Selhurst. Illustrated here No 5413 approaches Wandsworth Common on 13 August 1981 with a Victoria-Epsom Downs service. *Colin Marsden*

27
From the introduction of the 1982 winter timetable the majority of Central Division suburban services were operated by EPB type units, permitting a large number of ageing 4SUBs to be withdrawn. Facelift unit No 5404 passes through the Selhurst washing machine, situated at Norwood Junction, on 5 March 1982. *Colin Marsden*

28
Some SR designed 2EPB units have received facelift overhauls with the first six units being dealt with at Eastleigh works during 1982 and emerged carrying numbers 6301-6306. Set No 6301 is shown here arriving at Smitham station on 19 October 1982 on the Tattenham Corner branch with a train bound for Charing Cross. *Colin Marsden*

4CEP/4BEP

A total of 133 four-car main line units of the types 4BEP (4 coach Buffet Electro Pneumatic) and 4CEP (4 coach Corridor Electro Pneumatic) were built between 1957 and 1963, primarily for use on the South Eastern Division's Kent coast electrification system.

4CEP

The four-car CEP units were the first main line units built to the BR standard coach design and were basically a Mk I body, mounted on an EMU type underframe, fitted with electrical equipment and EP braking. Construction of the units was carried out at Eastleigh on frames from Ashford and these were the first of the 'modern' emus. Gangways were fitted throughout with Pullman style connections at the unit ends. Four prototype sets were built during 1956 and numbered 7101-7104, these were allocated to Brighton for use on the Central Division. The formation was MBSO (Motor Brake Second Open), TCK (Trailer Composite Corridor), TSK (Trailer Second Corridor), MBSO (Motor Brake Second Open). The total passenger accommodation provided was for 24 first and 200 second class passengers. The MBSO cars, which weighed 40 tonnes, contained a full width driving cab with access via the guard's compartment situated immediately behind. 56 second class passengers were carried in this vehcile which was divided into two three-bay saloons with a centre full width entrance corridor, access doors were also provided by vestibules at each end. The two trailer vehicles were both of similar design, one having three second, and four first class compartments, fed by a full length side corridor with a toilet at each end, this being classified as TCK; the other coach classified as a TSK also had a full length side corridor but the second class accommodation was provided in eight compartments with two toilets provided at the same end. Trailer coaches weighed 30-31 tonnes. Traction equipment carried was two English Electric 250hp traction motors mounted under the leading end of each MBSO car. The first four units were fitted with 1951 style electro-pneumatic contactor control equipment. Buckeye couplings were provided at the outer ends and between vehicles, on outer ends high-level air pipes were also fitted together with electrical control jumpers. To provide power for control and coach lighting a 70 volt motor generator (MG) set was fitted under the MBSO vehicles. As the first four prototype units proved highly successful a further production fleet was ordered during 1957/8 for service on the newly electrified Kent coast lines. These were numbered 7105-7153. This fleet was closely modelled on the earlier units but incorporated a number of modifications including the replacement of the EP contactor equipment with the latest type of 1957 camshaft control equipment, another change was that only one of the MBSO vehicles was fitted with an MG set. Other modifications were carried out to the bogies, brake equipment, sound insulation and heating. Inside the vehicles alterations were made to the upholstery style with plastic laminate replacing wood veneer on bulkhead panels, aluminium luggage racks were fitted in place of the strung type and double glazed windows were also fitted. As several units were completed prior to their required service, they were stored at Lancing, Gatwick, and on the 'Bluebell Branch' between Ardingly and Horsted Keynes, which at that time was being operated as a single line railway.

After the Kent Coast units had been in traffic for only a short time, complaints were received from railway staff and passengers regarding the units' rough riding, giving SR management some cause for concern. When the third batch of units for use on the second phase of the Kent coast electrification were ordered during 1960, the units were fitted with the Commonwealth all steel type bogie fitted with roller bearings, which greatly improved the ride. This third batch of units allocated running numbers 7154-7204 were of identical appearance to the previous fleet, and in fact continued the production run at Eastleigh, being delivered to traffic between August 1960 and September 1961. During 1962 a further seven units of the same design and numbered 7205-7211 were ordered for the South Western Division and delivered during 1963, however these did not operate on the SWD for many years and soon joined their elder sisters operating on the SED.

4BEP

To operate with the CEP units a fleet of BEP units was built, initially two were constructed to operate with the prototype sets and numbered 7001-7002. Construction was carried out alongside CEP units Nos 7101-7104 at Eastleigh and units were identical except that the TSK coach was replaced by a TRB (Trailer Restaurant Buffet), thus decreasing the second class seating to 132, but giving 21 unclassified seats in the buffet car. Power for the buffet vehicle was provided by a separate MG mounted on the underframe of the coach. When built, due to late delivery of the buffet cars, the two sets were put into traffic as three-car CEP formations. The next batch of buffet units numbered 7003-7012 were built in collaboration with CEP units Nos 7105-7153 for the Kent coast phase one electrification. These were fitted with camshaft control equipment and more modern interiors, in common with the CEP units of the build. For use on the second phase of the Kent coast electrification scheme a further 10 BEP units numbered 7013-7022 were ordered, these were constructed during early 1961 in line with CEP units Nos 7154-7204. An interesting fitting during the mid-1960s was an air conditioning system to the buffet car of unit No 7022, this was for evaluation purposes but was not fitted to subsequent units.

The allocation of units has mainly stayed consistent during their lives with the prototype sets Nos 7001-7002, 7101-7104 being allocated to Brighton for use on business trains when new, and remaining there for the best part of the next 20 years, before being allocated to Ramsgate. Units Nos 7105-7204 built for the Kent coast electrification programme together with buffet sets Nos 7003-7022 have operated in that area for the best part of their lives. Sets Nos 7205-7211 built for the SWD did not operate on this Division for many years and were soon to be found on the SED. On the SED units operated to most parts of the electrified main line sections and provided the stable power for many years. When built units were painted in green livery, that was subsequently changed to all blue on many units. From the late 1960s units have been painted in blue and grey livery. Under the BR numerical classification system of the 1970s CEP units became Class 411 and BEP units Class 410 being sub-classed 1 and 2 depending on their equipment, whether of 1951 or 1957 types.

With no new stock envisaged for many years during 1975 a Kent coast stock refurbishment programme was planned, which involved completely rebuilding these 20+ year old units from the frames upwards. As a prototype set No 7153 underwent extensive rebuilding at Eastleigh and emerged in its new form during November 1975, the new formation being DMS (Driving Motor Second), TBC (Trailer Brake Composite), TS (Trailer Second), DMS. This rebuilding had removed the brake van and guard's accommodation from the driving cars to a new central position, bringing the units more in line with the modern 1963 designed units. The former guard's compartment behind the driver's cab was replaced by a second class seating bay with the driver's cab being reached via a transverse gangway to the rear of the cab in common with more modern stock. The former TCK vehicle was converted to the new TBC, with two of the former three second class compartments being converted

29
When first introduced the 4CEP units were described by some people as a 'modern COR' and technically they were correct, but the units contained far more modern equipment with an up-to-date cab layout and were constructed to the latest building techniques. The second of the initial prototype order poses for the official photograph on 15 May 1956. Note the lion on wheel coat of arms. *British Railways*

into a guard's van with small office adjoining. The remaining second class compartment at the outer end of the coach remained together with its adjacent toilet. The former TSK car was rebuilt to fully open standards with its two toilets remaining. The revised layout meant that passenger accommodation was now for 24 first and 198 second class passengers, only two less than when the unit was in its original form but giving passengers a more pleasant environment. During the rebuilding of the prototype refurbished unit No 7153, modern upholstery and fluorescent lighting were fitted, but the original style windows were retained. Slight modification was carried out to the Pullman gangways on the unit ends and to improve the ride commonwealth bogies were fitted throughout except to the powered bogies. Following its release from Eastleigh works set No 7153 was the feature of much press and passenger attention and was shown off at numerous stations and depots throughout the region. The new appearance was widely accepted and a full refurbishment plan was authorised for the complete fleet. As Eastleigh was unable to cope with the large number of units involved and the BREL works at Swindon had spare capacity, it was decided that the programme should be undertaken there, meaning that all units had to be hauled to and from the Southern. Various alterations were made to the Swindon refurbished units namely the replacement of windows with the tinted glass drop hopper type. Originally all non-powered bogies were of the Commonwealth type but subsequent cost cutting has meant that later units have returned to SR mounted on their original bogies. Following the introduction of the first fully refurbished unit during 1979 a start was made to renumber these units in the BR six digit computer based system, therefore units emerged carrying the 411 prefix to their numbers, however the Southern soon decided to drop the first two digits and units are now referred to in the 15xx and 16xx range. As units were not outshopped from Swindon in any particular order it was decided to make a fresh start to numbering under the new system. Original 'prototype' units would become (41)1.501-(41)1.505; the phase one production units 7105-7153 would become (41)1.506-(41)1.564 and the phase two units (41)1.565-(41)1.620. This included 10 of the former BEP units where buffet cars have been replaced by converted loco-hauled trailer vehicles.

The 10 second phase BEP units however, are to be refurbished, the unit emerging during late 1982. The refurbishment of these BEP units has taken the same form as the CEP fleet. Numbering of the 10 buffet sets will be (41)2.301-(41)2.310. After arrival back on the SR the first refurbished buffet set, reclassified as Class 412, was transferred to Fratton for use on the Waterloo-Portsmouth line. For their trip to the works at Swindon units are normally sent to Strawberry Hill EMU depot under their own power from the SED. At Strawberry Hill shoe beams and traction equipment are removed and the units are then hauled with a Class 33/1 or 73 locomotive to Swindon. Being hauled as fitted vehicles, on their return testing is carried out at Strawberry Hill depot and on the Shepperton branch usually in connection with test unit No ADB975032 *MARS*. The rate of refurbishment during the initial period was about two units per month.

30
The first production fleet looked identical to the prototype batch and were numbered 7105-7153. The first of the series is seen here in an 'as built' condition, painted in green livery with the standard BR lion on wheel emblem on the body side. Coach and unit numbers are in yellow, but no first class yellow roof band is carried on the TCK vehicle at this time. *British Railways*

31
Construction of the CEP/BEP fleet was undertaken at the Eastleigh workshops with partly completed frames supplied by Ashford. This view shows an MBSO vehicle under construction, taken from the inner end of the car. The illustration was taken about 18 days into the build and shows the underframe and body ends in position, with underfloor pipe work being applied. *Author's Collection*

32
The four 'prototype' units were trimmed more in the style of the old COR units, here the MBSO vehicle is shown (from the driving end). Seats are arranged in the low-density 2+2 mode, with a centre gangway. Glass shaded reading lamps were provided above each pair of seats with an individual switch, aluminium roof luggage racks were also fitted. *British Railways*

33
The modern version of the SR BUF unit was the BEP (Buffet Electro-pneumatic). Buffet cars were equipped with a small counter for sundry purchases, a full sized kitchen and three bays of seats for passengers taking refreshment. Car No S69005 of unit No 7006 is shown here taken from the counter end. Under the buffet car was an additional motor generator and battery to provide power for the kitchen equipment. *P. J. Sharpe*

34
The modern kitchen was specially designed by GEC and consisted of a single oven range, grill toaster, and hot cupboard, with plenty of wall-mounted storage cupboards above, with a double stainless steel sink unit on the opposite side. *GEC Traction Ltd*

35
Such was the rate of construction of production units of the initial order that delivery overtook the demand, therefore during 1959 more than 20 sets were placed in store on the Copyhold Junction-Horsted Keynes branch (at that time regular services were using the branch as a single line). This view was taken on 17 May 1959 with set No 7128 nearest the camera. *R. C. Riley*

36
Although the units were intended for operation on the various phases of the Kent Coast electrification, during the 1960s several units saw service on the Central Division lines. Set No 7124, still painted in green livery, pulls out of Horsham with the 17.02 Victoria-Littlehampton (via Sutton and Dorking) service on 3 June 1964. *John Scrace*

37
Between the guard's compartment and passenger vestibule doors, clips were provided to carry destination boards. This view of 4BEP No 7008 at Faversham shows a destination board in use, although most photographic records show they were seldom used. *P. J. Sharpe*

38
When the SR introduced their fleet of six prototype electro-diesel locomotives during the early 1960s, one of the design features was the feasibility to couple to a modern emu formation in multiple and to drive from the emu remote cab but still fully controlling the locomotive. A further innovation was the braking system: the emu and locomotive would be using the automatic air/ep brake while in multiple, but if the locomotive was hauling a vacuum fitted train, equipment within the locomotive would automatically convert the braking system enabling both air and vacuum brakes to be controlled from the emu cab. Considerable testing and training had to be given in this field, and in the early 1960s a number of trains were operated on the SED. In this shot a 4CEP leads, with an electro-diesel (type JA) in the middle and a train of vacuum braked stock at the rear. *Stan Creer*

39
The SR, in common with all regions, commenced applying yellow warning panels from the mid-1960s to all emus, dmus and locomotives. Initially this was achieved on the CEP/BEP fleet by painting the lower half of the end vestibule door, but after a few years it became compulsory for a full yellow end. Set No 7200 passes Sandwich station on 28 January 1966 with a Charing Cross-Margate-Folkestone train. *Colin Marsden Collection*

40
The supply of main line units for the Central and South Eastern sections at Victoria is provided by Stewarts Lane (SL) depot. In this 1969 view of the depot a variety of liveries can be seen. From left to right: 4EPB No 5048 in green with yellow panel, 4CEP No 7119 in all blue with full yellow end, 4CEP No 7124 in modern inter-city colours, 2EPB No 5793 in green with full yellow end, SR 2HAP No 5621 in all blue with yellow warning end and 4CEP No 7194 in green, probably with a yellow warning panel. *GEC Traction Ltd*

41
A Ramsgate-Victoria service formed of a 4CEP/VEP formation climbs away from Rochester towards Sole Street during 1978, while on the down line a 4VEP forms a stopping service from Victoria to Gillingham. All main line units operating on the SED are allocated to Ramsgate depot, but sundry repairs can be carried out at a number of smaller locations. *Colin Marsden*

42
During the early 1980s with the refurbishment programme underway various reallocations were made to enable units requiring attention to be sent to works but still maintaining the correct number of units in traffic. Service cutbacks on the SR during 1981 meant that most remaining buffet services were withdrawn, rendering a number of BEP units redundant, however some units were put into traffic with de-stored buffet cars and operated CEP diagrams. BEP No 7014 operating as a 'non buffet' unit from Brighton approaches Streatham North Junction with a Victoria-Brighton service on 4 March 1982. *Colin Marsden*

43
For several years prior to the refurbishing programme the early prototype CEP/BEP units operated from Brighton depot and were seen regularly on CD main line services. No 7101 hurries a Victoria-Littlehampton service between Clapham Junction and Wandsworth Common on 19 November 1979. *Colin Marsden*

44
During early 1975 set No 7153 entered Eastleigh works for a general overhaul and whilst undergoing this repair was completely refurbished, serving as a prototype of what could possibly be carried out to the rest of the fleet. After refurbishment the unit took part in numerous exhibitions before returning to traffic on the SED. No 7153 is seen here with an Ashford-Charing Cross slow service near Ashford on 15 May 1980. *Colin Marsden*

45
CEP No 7155 leading a VEP/CEP formation works a Victoria-Dover Western Docks train through the lovely Kent countryside between Pluckley and Ashford, during the summer of 1981. The roof mounted guard's periscopes are visible on the leading unit, a feature which has been removed from refurbished sets. *Colin Marsden*

46
A shop full of SR emu stock is a slight change from the Swindon Works 'A' shop of the past, where main line steam and diesel locomotives were built and serviced. During the Kent Coast refurbishment programme it was normal for approximately 6-8 units to be in the works at any one time, with each unit staying for some three months. Here various cars of units Nos (41)1.515, (41)1.601 and (41)1.600 take shape. *British Railways*

47
A new traverser was installed at Swindon for use during the emu refurbishment programme enabling easy access to all the shop bays. MBSO No S61695 of unit No 7154 awaits entry to the shop for stripping, upon return to SR this car was part of set No (41)1.606. *British Railways*
British Railways

48
It was the intention that when refurbished units returned to traffic they would bear the new six figure TOPS based number, and indeed the first 27 units to return to traffic received this treatment. However the SR's reluctance to depart from the four-figure system resulted in subsequent units carrying only the last four numbers. On their return to SR sets pass through Strawberry Hill where recommissioning takes place. Set No 411.510 stands alongside new Class 508 No 508.028 inside the shed on 10 May 1980. *Colin Marsden*

49
From late 1980 passenger trains on the SED were formed of a mixture of refurbished and unrefurbished sets often within the same train. Passenger reaction was not favourable and complaints of uncomfortable seats, doors that did not fit and were the cause of draughts, and even water dripping through the roofs, were not uncommon. Set No 411.515 leads a 12-car formation past Petts Wood on 6 February 1982 with a Charing Cross-Margate service.
Colin Marsden

50
It was noted at Charing Cross that if mixed formations were in traffic during the peak period passengers would pass by the refurbished unit and prefer to sit in the old unit, even if it was overcrowded, however from late 1982 only a handful of unrefurbished sets remained in traffic and the public had little alternative but to use the newer sets. No 411.513 descends from Polehill Tunnel towards Dunton Green with a Victoria-Folkestone Harbour service on 4 June 1982.
Colin Marsden

51
The refurbishment programme for the Class 411/410 units is due for completion by the end of 1983 when the SR will have a fleet of units capable of providing a satisfactory passenger service for the next 20 years. Set No 1538 formerly No 7112, passes through the Kent countryside to the south of Paddock Wood with a Charing Cross-Folkestone/Margate service on 4 June 1982.
Colin Marsden

52
The first of the refurbished 4BEP units reclassified as 412 arrived on the SR during December 1982, the number allocated was 412.301, which was formerly set No 7019. The buffet car had been completely rebuilt with a bar and standing room only, three bays of 2+2 seating being provided at the opposite end, but not purposely dedicated to buffet use. Car No S69341, formerly S69018, stands at Waterloo during an inspection. *Colin Marsden*

2HAP/2SAP/4CAP

The Southern Region's two-car HAP stock can be separated into two categories, 1) those built to Bulleid SR design and 2) those built to BR all steel standard design.

Although both types emerged from the Southern's carriage works at Eastleigh at approximately the same time, we will first deal with the SR designed units, of which there were 36, all built on reclaimed frames from 2NOL units. Construction of the HAPs commenced during 1956 and five units carrying running numbers 5601-5605 emerged the following year; the remainder carrying running numbers 5606-5636 were placed into traffic during 1958. The formation of the units was MBSO (Motor Brake Second Open) and DTCL (Driving Trailer Composite with Lavatory). MBSO vehicles closely resembled the power cars formed in SR EPB units introduced during the early 1950s, and indeed during more recent years several MBSO cars have been used in the Class 415/4 facelift programme. The only internal difference between the MBSO cars used in EPB sets and the HAPs was that in the latter, the vehicle was divided into two four-bay sections. The DTCL vehicles had one full width half-compartment directly behind the driver's full width cab, the rest of the coach being fed via a side corridor with four compartments for second class occupation and three for first class, giving total car seating of 18 first and 38 second. Passenger access doors were provided from each compartment, and opposite each compartment door on the corridor side, except for the inner end compartment. Coach numbers carried were MBSOs — 14521-14556 and DTCLs — 16001-16036. The external appearance of the units conformed to the standard EPB or 1951 look, and all units were fitted with standard dropable buckeye couplings at the outer ends, with standard high level air and control jumpers. Between the two coaches a three link coupling being provided and a centre single buffer. When built units were intended for use on the new Thanet electrification programme and were allocated for routine maintenance at the emu depot of Slade Green. An interesting point worth noting is that these were the only Bulleid designed units to be fitted with express gear ratio, a feature now removed. Units remained operating on the SED until 1969 when the Southern Region had a mass reorganisation of emu stock which brought units 5602/5/7-9/15-18/22/34/35 to the SWD for use on the Waterloo-Windsor/Weybridge line. Once on the SWD the units had their first class accommodation declassified and the units were re-classified as SAPs. After one year of service with first class arm rests sewn up, carpets removed and toilets locked out of use, the SR Board decided on yet another use for the stock and during 1970 all were re-allocated to Brighton for use on the 'Coastway' line (between Portsmouth and Brighton), and whilst used in this area the first class accommodation was restored. The units normally operated in pairs on the 'Coastway' line until 1976 when further stock allocation alterations brought the units back to the London area for use on the Central suburban system with again the declassification of the first class seating. Soon after returning to the London area a refurbishing plan was drawn up for the 4EPB units and as a prototype for this, two units Nos 5601/36 were disbanded and their motor coaches formed with redundant SUB trailers into a new 4EPB unit numbered 5263 (late 5401). Following this successful reforming several units have now been disbanded and formed into new EPB units during the early 1980s, each time giving way to the withdrawal of the DTCL vehicle as this is non-standard to operating requirements. The livery applied to units when built was standard emu green, yellow warning panels were later added, and when they were, the black triangle on the cab end under the route indicator panel on the DMBS vehicles also appeared, denoting to operating staff that the guard's van was at the end of the train. In more recent years standard rail blue livery has been applied and during the early 1980s some units have been painted in Inter-City livery. Traction equipment is of the standard type, in the form of two 250hp English Electric traction motors mounted on the leading bogie of the MBSO. Under the BR class system units were classified 418.

At approximately the same time as the 56xx HAP units were under construction a much larger fleet of BR designed HAP units were being developed at Eastleigh as replacement power for the aged HAL stock on the SED Gillingham and Maidstone lines. The first unit carrying running number 6001 emerged from Eastleigh during June 1957 and visually was practically identical to the 57xx 2EPB units already constructed, in fact the MBSO vehicles were the same except that express gear ratios were fitted to the HAP series. The basic formation of these units followed the early 56xx type with each unit formed of a MBSO and DTCL vehicle, however the internal layout of the DTCL car was greatly revised and now in place of having the side corridor along the whole coach with a toilet at one end, the first and second class accommodation was divided by two centre toilets, with three first class compartments, with side corridor directly behind the driver's position, and a five bay second class saloon at the opposite end. In the MBSO, passenger accommodation is in two saloons of four bays, each two-car unit having a total seating capacity of 19 first and 134 second. The first 42 units of the fleet were built with the older (1951) style electro-pneumatic control equipment, whilst all subsequent units were fitted with the more modern (1957) camshaft control equipment. Often the two types of unit are referred to by operating staff as either 1951 or 1957 stock, depending on the type of equipment carried. By the end of 1958 all 42 units of the first order were in traffic and soon a further order for 63 units was placed. These were to operate on the Thanet lines and were allocated running numbers 6043-6105. For the second phase of the Kent coast electrification in 1961 a further fleet of HAP units were ordered and these were allocated running numbers 6106-6146. The final batch of HAPs came during 1962/3 when 27 units were introduced for use on the South Western and Central Divisions, running numbers allocated were 6147-6173. Although all the batches are of identical internal layout, apart from a few minor cab and internal fitments, the various builds can be recognised mainly by roof detail. Early units of the 1951 type have a mass of exterior cabling on the roof while the early 1957 builds have plain roofs except for the compartment air ventilators. Later 1957 builds are fitted with rainwater strips at an angle above the cant rail. During their life the HAPs have operated on all three divisions of the SR and have visited most corners of the system. The fleet remained wholly intact until 1973 when due to a shortage of suburban stock it was decided to downgrade a fleet of BR standard HAPs to SAPs in the same way as that previously done to the SR designed units. The downgraded units were Nos 6001-6021/6024-6044 which became 5901-5942 and were intended for use on the Waterloo-Windsor/Weybridge service, but as time came to prove these units were more widely used mostly on the SWD. Units Nos 6022/3 were not downgraded as at the time they were taking part in rolling stock development tests with 'Tightlock' couplings. This was in fact the prototype equipment for the 1972 designed high density stock couplings. Further alterations to the Southern's stock allocations resulted in downgraded units being returned to their HAP status during 1979/80. BR classification for the HAPs is 414 while those converted to SAPs were classified 418. During 1982, to give the 'Coastway' route fixed four coach formations with the guard's van in the centre of the formation, a fleet of 4CAP units were formed, utilising two 2HAP units semi-permanently coupled motor coach to motor coach, one guard's van being converted to a luggage van, with certain technical equipment removed as were the two intermediate driving cabs. After their introduction into service the first class accommodation in one set was declassified. The only alteration to the coupling between the two units was the removal of the buckeye release chains from the buffer beams, to avoid nintentional uncoupling. As part of the 4CAP fleet was to be formed of 1951 style units and the others from those fitted with 1957 equipment, two separate sub-sections to the fleet were formed, classified as 413/2 and 413/3 and numbered 3201-3212 and 3301-3311 respectively, all units being allocated to Brighton. An interesting point is that during reformation of the units which took place on a random basis, no consideration was given to the livery carried, and in several cases units were in traffic with two coaches painted in all blue and two in Inter-City livery. From the introduction of the 1982 summer service some 30 units were withdrawn from service, some being converted to departmental use while the majority went to scrap. At the time of going to press the current allocation for the remaining HAP units is Wimbledon 24 units and Ramsgate 65 units.

53
Displaying 'as built' livery, HAP No 6107, destined for the second phase of the Kent coast electrification, stands outside Eastleigh works immediately after completion but prior to shoe gear being fitted. This view is taken from the DTC (Driving Trailer Composite) end. Note the commonwealth bogies at the inner end of both vehicles.
British Railways

54
With MBSO leading set No 6053 approaches Chislehurst with a Charing Cross-Margate line train on 30 June 1959. This unit was one of the second batch, introduced for the Thanet line. When this illustration was taken the unit sported large headcode numerals and whistle (mounted above the driver's window). *British Railways*

55
When the BR fleet of HAP units entered service they were painted in standard green livery with no frontal warning panel, however these were added during the mid-1960s. Set No 6089 in original condition leads an eight-car formation of BR HAP stock on the SED with a Margate line train during 1961. Unit and carriage numbers were applied in yellow at this time. *Colin Marsden Collection*

56
The final batch of units to be constructed, Nos 6147-73 were intended for the SWD but after only a short period they were to be seen in operation on the SED in company with the various Kent coast electrification batches. No 6155 with yellow warning panel stands at Martin Mill on 4 September 1968 with the 11.10 Margate-Charing Cross. *John Scrace*

57
Following the introduction of the Bournemouth electrification in 1967 many unusual formations could be recorded; one interesting combination during that summer was the 10.47 Swanage-Waterloo which was formed of hauled TC stock. The train is seen here on 15 July approaching Basingstoke hauled by 2HAP No 6058 with Class 73 No E6012 in the middle of the formation, providing extra power. *John Faulkner*

58
As will be seen by this illustration, the SR build of HAPs resembled the SR EPBs in nearly every way, and indeed in later years the majority of units have given their MBSO vehicles to 'new' 4EPB units. Sporting early blue livery set No 5608 leading a formation of SR/BR HAP stock operates on the SED during September 1966. It is interesting to note that when painted in early blue livery unit numbers were smaller than those carried today and the coach number was placed under the cab window. *British Railways*

59
Following a mishap SR designed HAP No 5624 (downgraded to a SAP) acquired a BR standard design MBSO during the early 1980s, thus giving an unusual appearance of SR/BR vehicles formed in the same unit. Set No 5624 is seen here departing from Clapham Junction with a Victoria-Beckenham Junction service on 12 August 1981, with the BR MBSO leading. *Colin Marsden*

60
At the beginning of the 1980s SR designed units were downgraded to second class accommodation only and were thus reclassified as 2SAP units, all being allocated to Selhurst and operating along with EPB units on Central Division suburban services. Mass withdrawals of the class commenced during 1982 when over half of the fleet were disbanded and sent to Horwich works as part of the Class 415 facelift programme. Set No 5615 approaches Streatham North Junction on 4 March 1982 with a Victoria-Coulsdon North service. *Colin Marsden*

61
Services on the London Bridge (CD) suburban section also utilised these 56xx SR designed SAP units during the early 1980s. Approaching Bromley Junction a London Bridge-Epsom Downs service is formed of four units, the leading one repainted in standard inter-city colours. In this view the former DTC, now a DTS vehicle, is leading. *Colin Marsden*

62
During the early 1970s HAP units Nos 6022 and 6023 were fitted with tightlock couplings the same as those used on modern high density emu stock. For testing purposes the units lost their conventional buffing and draw-gear at one end and the experimental low level couplings were fitted, visible here on the DTC vehicle of unit No 6023 at Aldershot on 14 July 1976. *Ray Ruffell*

63
During recent years the HAP fleet has been allocated to Ramsgate, Brighton and Wimbledon. Brighton allocated units normally being used on 'Coastway' services with occasional appearances on London stopping services. Set No 6036 passes Three Bridges on 22 February 1982 with a London Bridge-Brighton train. *Colin Marsden*

64
Former tightlock coupling fitted HAP No 6023 passes Lewes signalbox and enters the station with a Seaford-Brighton local service during the summer of 1979. From 1982 the majority of CD allocated HAP units were semi-permanently coupled in pairs and reclassified as 4CAP (Coastway HAP units). *Colin Marsden*

65
South Western allocated units are often used to supplement 'main line' trains during peak periods, when trains of eight and ten coaches are required. On 21 July 1980 set No 6016 leads a Guildford-Waterloo via Cobham service away from Guildford. Guildford's University and Cathedral can be seen in the background. *Andrew French*

66
The different batches of HAP units are usually recognisable apart, mainly by roof details. The final batch of units Nos 6147-6173 introduced during 1962/3 have roof mounted angled rain water strips, clearly visible in this view. This fleet of units was also fitted with smaller headcode boxes. No 6150 nears Staplehurst on 15 May 1980 with an Ashford-Charing Cross stopping service. *Colin Marsden*

67
When the BRB high speed track recording car No DB999550 visited the SR during May 1981 the vehicle was marshalled between two 2HAP units with a Class 73 locomotive on the rear end. In this illustration taken on 15 May, HAPs Nos 6098 and 6103 with test car between and Class 73 No 73.101 *Brighton Evening Argus* at the rear, approaches Woking with the 06.00 Eastleigh-Alton test train. *Andrew French*

68
The train now standing *on* Platform 12 is 2HAP No 6167! This interesting photograph was taken at London Bridge soon after an arriving train split the points at the entrance to the platform and landed up straddled half on the track and partly on the platform itself. It is a wonder the vehicle did not topple over on to its side. *British Railways*

69
To provide the SWD with additional two-car all second class units during the late 1970s, HAPs 6001-6021, and 6024-6052 were down-graded. This was done by sewing up the first class compartment arm-rests, locking the toilet out of use and renumbering the units in the 59xx range. An eight-car formation formed of two 2SAPs and two 2HAPs pass Hampton Court Junction on 4 April 1980 with the 10.43 Hampton Court-Waterloo service. *Colin Marsden*

70
A six-car formation of SAP stock approaches Clapham Junction on the Windsor lines, with a Waterloo-Waterloo via Twickenham and Hounslow service on 19 November 1979. Wandsworth Town station can be seen in the background, with a 4CIG unit on the up main line forming a Reading-Waterloo service. Three non-electrified sidings that form an extension of Clapham Junction Yard are seen on the left. *Colin Marsden*

71

By the middle of 1980 the majority of down-graded units were returned to their dual class status, and by 1981 many of the fleet were outshopped by Selhurst and the main works at Eastleigh in Inter-City blue-grey livery, displayed here on WD allocated unit No 6013, standing outside its home depot. *Colin Marsden*

72

The HAP fleet have appeared in many guises over the years and during 1982 a fleet of CAP units were formed by semi-permanently coupling two 2HAPs together, with their MBSO vehicles in the middle. Two different batches were formed — those fitted with 1951 style equipment which were classified 413/2 and numbered in the 32xx range, and those with the more modern 1957 style equipment 413/3 and numbered in the 33xx range. Standing at Barnham on the Coastway line, the route for which the units were converted, are sets Nos 3311 and 3201 on 7 June 1982.
Colin Marsden

73
After initial conversion work which included the removal of some cab equipment from the inner cabs and the reclassification of a guard's van to a luggage compartment, units entered service from Brighton depot with first class accommodation in both driving trailer cars, however this proved to be too generous for the Coastway route and soon one vehicle was downgraded to all second class accommodation. Set No 3302 approaches Portcreek Junction with a Brighton-Portsmouth train on 12 June 1982. *Colin Marsden*

74
Soon after introduction as a CAP unit set No 3306 arrives at the Coastway terminus of Eastbourne while working the 15.42 Ore-Brighton service on 4 August 1982. The patch around the unit number gives away that when reformed the unit was not repainted, and that only the number was replaced. *Colin Marsden*

MLV/TLV

After the implementation of the Kent coast electrification scheme it was an obvious operational improvement if the London-Dover boat trains were operated by emu formations, but it was soon found that the luggage space on the CEP/BEP formations operating the route was inadequate. Initially two MLV (Motor Luggage Vans) were constructed to operate on the Kent coast phase 1 electrification. The vans were 67ft 1in long and were built at Eastleigh, driving cabs were provided at each end and in between was a large and small luggage area, together with a small guard's coupé. Three double opening doors were provided each side, enabling most luggage to be readily loaded including palletised traffic by forklift trucks. Traction equipment was two 250hp English Electric traction motors, together with standard EP brake equipment, enabling the single cars to operate with any multiple-unit of the 1951/57/63/66 type. A special feature for which the units are renowned is the fitting of a 230amp/h traction battery giving sufficient power to enable the vehicle to operate locally off the electrified area, such as into quayside sidings or on dock lines. As the vehicles were designed to operate with vacuum braked goods stock, a vacuum exhauster was fitted enabling the haulage of a short vacuum fitted train. If a vacuum fitted train was required to be hauled away from the electrified area 100 tons trailing is the maximum load permitted. Ends of cars were fitted with standard dropable buckeye couplings and high level air and control pipes, and at buffer beam level a vacuum pipe, unique to any emu vehicle. Following the introduction of the second phase of the Kent coast electrification scheme that would take electric trains

75
Running under traction battery conditions two MLVs Nos 68005 and 68004 run on to the quayside line at Dover Marine, after arrival as part of the 09.00 Victoria-Dover-Ostend boat train on 3 March 1961. The livery when this illustration was taken was standard green. As these vehicles were numbered in the coaching stock series no unit numbers were allocated, but in recent years the car number has been applied to the front. *M. Edwards*

to Folkestone and the Harbour branch, a further batch of eight MLV cars were constructed to an identical design. No unit numbers have ever been allocated to the MLVs but during more recent years the car numbers 68001-68010 have been applied to vehicle ends in the same manor as unit numbers on emu trains. In common with other emu stock, the livery applied when built was green, which subsequently altered to rail blue and grey during the late 1960s. All vehicles were allocated to Ramsgate when new and have remained there , normally operating with CEP and BEP stock.

After several years of operation it was found that with high season boat train traffic, one luggage van was insufficient for the loadings and between 1963 and 1968 it was not uncommon for boat trains from the channel ports to Victoria to be formed of two luggage vans leading a train of 12CEP. The result was during 1968 six conventional BG (Brake Gangway) luggage vans were fitted with EP braking and high level air and emu jumper cables, to act as TLVs (Trailer Luggage Vans). The conversion work from BG to TLV was carried out by the Southern's CM & EE staff at Selhurst and during the conversion work the end corridor connections were retained but sealed out of use. These were retained in case the cars ever returned to loco-hauled status. The livery applied when converted was BR maroon, which subsequently changed to standard Inter-City blue and grey.

Following the general decline in luggage carried on the coast routes the six TLVs were taken out of service early in 1975 and stored, first at Eastleigh and then at Oatlands Cutting, near Walton-on-Thames, before being used as match wagons for the second batch of REP and TC stock from York Works to the SR. After this was completed during 1976 the vehicles were again stored and subsequently converted during 1979 into HST en-parts wagons to operate between the BREL works at Doncaster and the WR sheds.

76

Formed as the lead vehicle of a Dover Western Docks-Victoria boat train, MLV No 68002 heads a twelve-car formation of CEP/BEP stock on the approaches to Ashford during the early 1960s. When running under these conditions the MLV would be taking power from the third-rail, at the same time replenishing power in the cars' traction batteries. *P. J. Sharpe*

77

The TLV vehicles introduced during 1968 are not commonly photographed but this view taken at Sandling shows MLV No 68009 (painted in standard blue-grey livery with car number on the front) leading a TLV on a Dover-Victoria boat train. It is rare for emu formations to normally exceed 12 cars, but when MLV and TLV vehicles were used formations of up to 14 vehicles were not uncommon. *G. Roy-Hounsell*

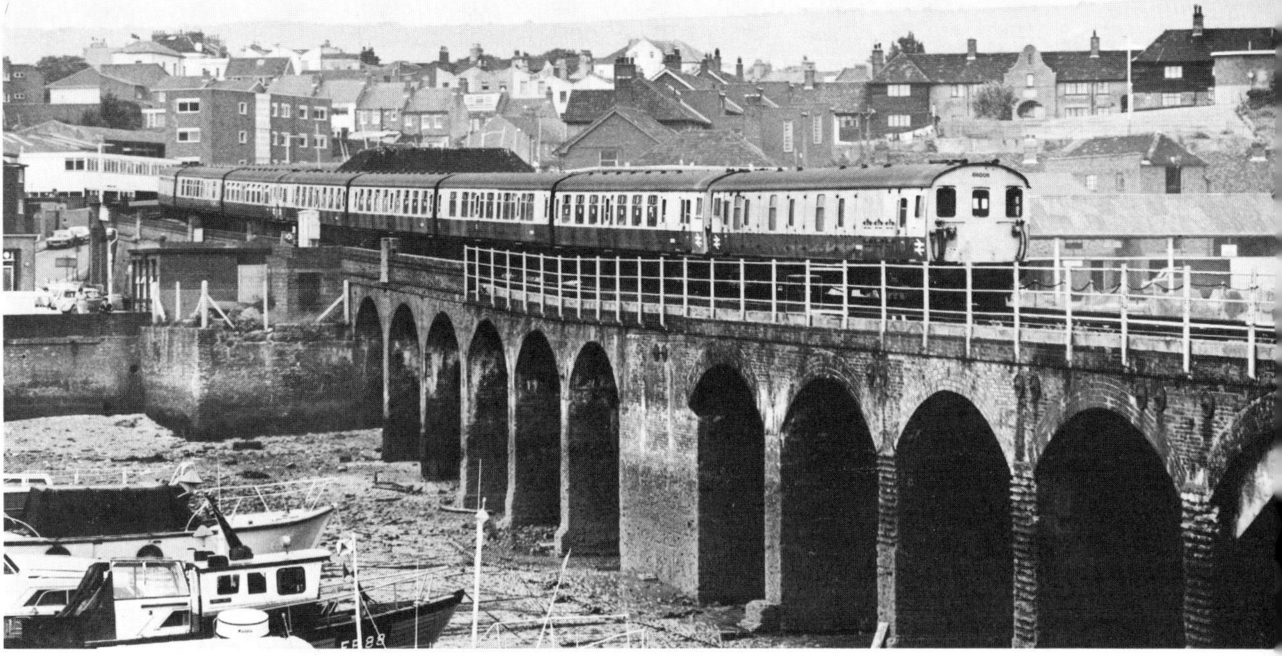

78
It is not only boat train services to Dover that operate with MLV vehicles in the formations. To provide additional luggage space on Victoria-Folkestone Harbour workings MLVs are used, these are always marshalled at the London end of trains to enable ease in loading and unloading at Victoria and is also more convenient at the Docks.
No 68008 approaches Folkestone Harbour with a train of continental bound passengers on 3 June 1982.
Colin Marsden

79
MLV in close-up: Driving positions are provided at each end, fitted with standard emu controls, plus additional equipment for operation of the vacuum brake exhauster and traction battery equipment. In between is a guard's compartment with both a large and small luggage van. The hinged body panels at the far end give access to the traction batteries.
No 68009 stands outside Stewarts Lane on 5 August 1981. *Colin Marsden*

80
MLVs are provided with standard traction equipment in the form of two English Electric 250hp traction motors, thus making a total of 3,500hp available for the 13-car formation. No 68008 leads a Folkestone Harbour-Victoria boat express at Cheriton on 3 June 1982. *Colin Marsden*

81
The nose end connections of MLVs are standard for all units constructed after 1951 except for PEP, Class 455 and Class 508 sets, thus enabling the MLV fleet to operate in multiple with a large variety of classes, however they are seldom seen in operation with anything other than Class 410/411 Kent Coat units. Under BR's numerical classification system MLVs were given Class 419. No 68006 is seen here at Folkestone Harbour on the rear of an up Folkestone-Victoria boat train. *Colin Marsden*

4CIG/4BIG

During the early 1960s the life expectancy of Southern Region main line electric stock was not foreseen as more than 5-7 years at the outside, and during 1962/3 plans were drawn up for a new generation of main line electric multiple-unit train. At the design stage it became apparent that a break from Southern tradition was to be made and that the powered vehicle was no longer to be a driving car and positioned at the end of the set, but was to be a vehicle containing the guard's van and traction equipment in the middle of the set. At the time when orders were being placed for this Brighton line replacement stock, the former Southern carriage works at Eastleigh had recently closed and the workshop at York was chosen to perform the building of this new stock, not a surprising choice as this works had been renowned for its coach building for many years. The new units were to be four-car sets, with a corridor throughout and Pullman style gangways at the outer ends. The initial order was for 36 4CIG (4-car Corridor Intermediate Gangway) units, and 18 4BIG (4-car Buffet Intermediate Gangway) sets. The formations were thus: 4CIG: DTC — Driving Trailer Composite, MBS — Motor Brake Second, TS — Trailer Second, DTC. On the 4BIG units the formation was the same but the TS vehicle was replaced by a TRB (Trailer Buffet). The DTC vehicles had a driver's position which only occupied half the width of the unit end with the handbrake controls in a vestibule on the opposite side, behind the driver's position was a full width vestibule for cab access. The passenger accommodation was set out for first class directly behind the driver in three or four compartments (each unit being formed of one DTC containing three, and 1 four First Class compartments), with the remaining compartment in the three first class compartment DTC for second class occupation, but to first class dimensions. Second class accommodation in the DTC vehicles was provided in three 2+2 seating bays (one of which had a door position) with two toilets situated at the inner end of the coach. The MBS vehicle contained a small luggage (security) cage with guard's office adjoining. Passenger accommodation was provided in $6\frac{1}{2}$ bays set out in the low density mode of 2+2 except behind the guard's office where there was a single line of six seats. Passenger access doors were provided in one seating bay and via an end vestibule. The power equipment mounted under this vehicle consisted of 4×250hp English Electric traction motors, two mounted on each bogie. The TS coach is basically a standard Mk 1 TSO vehicle built to emu requirements providing seating for 72 passengers in nine bays of eight. This gives a total passenger loading for the CIG unit of 42 first and 192 second. In BIG formations the buffet car accommodates 40 passengers in the second class seating mode, thus reducing the passenger capacity of these sets by 32. The external appearance of units was not dissimilar to the CEP/BEP units of 1959 vintage, but various body refinements were incorporated. On the front a revised Pullman gangway was fitted, while the high level air and control jumper cables were inset into the body panelling. Construction of this new generation emu stock, known to operating staff as 1963 stock, commenced at York during 1963 with the first unit carrying running number 7301 emerging during late 1964, with the final unit of the batch No 7336 not being completed until January 1966. The BIG variants allocated numbers 7031-7048 were not constructed until late 1965 and when the first CIG units were introduced, buffet accommodation was borrowed from the SED in the shape of 4BEP units. Once the first CIG unit was on the Southern a large staff training programme commenced not only to include drivers and guards but also depot staff, station staff and the supervisory grades, as this style of unit formed with a power car in the middle was completely new to the region. The first train to operate in passenger service formed of these new units was the 08.20 Brighton-London Bridge and 17.02 return to Eastbourne/Seaford on 29 March 1965. An interesting feature unique to CIG units 7301-7336 and BIG units 7031-7048 was an electric parking brake. In the cab the driver had two toggle switches marked 'Park brake apply' and 'Park brake release', these operated motors on the motor coach bogies which applied the brakes to the wheels of that coach, a duplicate set of controls also being provided in the guard's office.

Passenger reaction to these units was monitored closely and proved favourable. On the staff side units were proving successful with more driver comfort, less cab draughts and noise and a low failure rate. During the early years of use, due to lack of crew knowledge the units did not stray far from the Brighton-London route and even today the earlier units are seldom seen far away from the Central Division.

Towards the end of the 1960s the ageing 4COR/BUF units on the Waterloo-Portsmouth line were up for replacement, and a further fleet of CIG and BIG units were ordered for this route. Detail modifications were carried out including removal of the electric parking brake and re-designing of the driving cab equipment. In the passenger saloons and compartments the original units based on the CEP/BEP design had much wood veneer, but the second generation utilised modern plastic laminates and aluminium for internal decor. Externally the units followed the earlier Brighton line sets, exception being the fitting of differently designed bogies, and the guard's periscope carried on earlier units were now dispensed with. Again construction was carried out at York and unit numbering was followed on, CIGs becoming Nos 7337-7366 and BIGs Nos 7049-7058. As no new stock was available for outer suburban routes the 4COR units displaced from the Portsmouth route were found work operating on the Waterloo-Reading/Guildford via Ascot line and also on the Brighton 'Coastway' route until new stock could be made available. During 1969 a further order for 71 CIG units was issued as replacement stock for these ageing COR units. The new stock was delivered during 1970-72 with the appearance of units being identical to the earlier sets. Running numbers allocated to this batch were 7367-7437. Towards the end of the production run the SR was short of one main line unit (4CEP 7181 that had been withdrawn following a collision) and to cover this stock deficiency an additional CIG unit was ordered which became No 7438.

The CIG/BIG fleet took over all previous duties between London and the South Coast operated by COR/BUF/GRI/PAN and PUL units and worked to a very high standard. Central Division allocated units have always been allocated to Brighton, whilst those operating on the South Western Division worked from Fratton. When constructed units built to the initial order were painted in green livery, which was later changed to all blue, and subsequently to blue and grey, whilst units of the second and subsequent batches were delivered in standard Inter-City blue-grey livery.

Under the BR numerical class system 4CIG/BIG units became Class 421/420 respectively, the earlier electric park brake units forming sub-class 1 and later sets sub-class 2.

From May 1983 4CIG units were used to form two 8MIG sets for the Waterloo-Portsmouth line. Each MIG (Micro-buffet, CIG unit) was formed of a normal 4CIG, one of the MU fitted RMBs and a CIG with the TS removed. The units were renumbered 2601-2 and classified as 482.

82
One of the first public viewings of the modern '1963' style emus built as replacement for the ageing Brighton main line stock, was on 1 October 1964 when the pioneer 4CIG No 7301 painted in green livery with small yellow warning panel, was displayed at Waterloo. Until it went into passenger service in March 1965 the unit was occupied with crew training. *J. C. Haydon*

83
Although CIG units commenced operation from Brighton during March 1965, the 4BIG buffet units were not constructed until the autumn of that year. Delivery and testing took place during early 1966 and units did not enter passenger service until the summer of that year. In this photograph taken on 22 June 1966 set No 7039 departs from Haywards Heath with a Victoria service.
British Railways

84
The initial batch of 18 BIG units were all delivered by the end of 1966 and painted in green livery with small yellow warning panels. In line with the COR/BUF sets that these units replaced, roof destination board clips were provided, but were rarely used. Set No 7041 approaches Goring-by-Sea during 1967. *John Vaughan*

85
To many enthusiasts the CIG/BIG fleet looked their best in green livery, but alas only the first 36 CIG and 18 BIG units were outshopped in this style. Here a 12-car formation of CIG/BIG/CIG stock passes through the pleasant scenery of Wandsworth Common with the 10.45 Victoria-Eastbourne/Ore train on 28 May 1966. *John Scrace*

86
One of the strongholds for the CIG/BIG/CIG fleet is on the Waterloo-Portsmouth line. The fast services depart from Waterloo at 48 minutes past each hour usually formed of a CIG/BIG/CIG, and the 18 minutes past the hour service is formed just of CIG stock. The 09.48 Waterloo-Portsmouth Harbour is seen here approaching Guildford on 13 May 1982 led by unit No 7409. *Colin Marsden*

87
SWD CIG/BIG stock is maintained at Fratton where during late 1982 44 CIG and 8 BIG units were allocated. A fast Waterloo-Portsmouth Harbour service approaches Surbiton on a sunny spring day during 1980. It is usual operating practice to marshal the BIG unit in the centre of the formation. *Colin Marsden*

88
Apart from operating on the Waterloo-Portsmouth line, CIG stock share duties with VEP units on Waterloo-Reading, Guildford and Alton services. It is unusual to find CIG stock on other duties, however due to severe weather conditions on 24 January 1979 a CIG/VEP formation was employed on a Waterloo-Hampton Court service, seen here departing from Surbiton on its return trip to Waterloo. *Colin Marsden*

89
During the peak periods several Waterloo-Alton services stop at all stations south of Surbiton; these trains are often formed of CIG stock or a mixture of CIG and other main line units. No 7419 leads a VEP unit out of Weybridge on 11 May 1980 with the 16.52 service from Waterloo. *Colin Marsden*

WINTHROP
30
70

7419
53
7419

90
Running minus its BIG formation a Portsmouth Harbour-Waterloo fast service passes West Byfleet station on 8 April 1980. As mentioned in the introductory text the two driving vehicles of CIG/BIG units are of a different internal layout, one having four first class compartments while the other has only three, the remaining compartment being used by second class passengers. The vehicle with three first class compartments leads in this illustration. *Colin Marsden*

91
Passing a section of newly laid track on the down line, 4CIG No 7352 traverses the up line under full power as it climbs away from Liss towards Liphook on 19 May 1978. The section of line between Guildford and Portsmouth is heavily graded and curved causing severe problems with slipping during the autumn leaves season with numerous services having to be assisted in the winter months. *Colin Marsden*

92
Fleets of CIG units ordered at the beginning of 1969 and delivered from late 1970, were intended to replace COR units on their few remaining Portsmouth line services, and on the Waterloo-Reading/Guildford route. Over the years however the actual sets concerned have been interchanged, but CIG stock is still to be found operating on these routes. No 7416 stands at Aldershot on 18 April 1981 with the 09.34 Guildford-Waterloo via Ascot service. *Colin Marsden*

93
On the morning of 23 February 1979 an 8SUB formation running off the Hampton Court branch at Hampton Court Junction was in side-long collision with an Alton/Bournemouth-Waterloo semi-fast service. The SUB stock was derailed and pushed down an embankment, while the rear vehicle of the Alton/Bournemouth-Waterloo train lost its rear bogie and was dragged along the track for over a quarter of a mile before being brought to a stand; fortunately no one was seriously hurt. The CIG car involved No S76844 of unit No 7423 was taken to Slade Green for repairs and did not return to traffic until early 1982. The car is seen here mounted on a trolley bogie in the yard at Surbiton after removal from the accident scene. *Colin Marsden*

94
When odd vehicles of main line stock require moving between depots it is often achieved by coupling the vehicle to another emu. The interesting formation shown here of a CIG driving car coupled to a two and four car EPB was taken at Clapham Junction yard on 9 July 1979, when the CIG vehicle was being moved from Slade Green to Brighton via the SWD and Fratton. *Colin Marsden*

95
The Central Division was the first section of the SR to receive CIG/BIG units and still operate a sizeable fleet that are now in charge of the majority of CD main line services. Set No 7332 passes Clapham Junction during June 1981 with a Victoria-Brighton semi-fast service. *Colin Marsden*

7373
7373
2
7725
7725
08

96
This view serves as a good comparison between the CIG and VEP units and shows that from the front end there are no detail differences to assist recognition except in the number range. The two trains are shown approaching Wandsworth Common and are, on the left 4CIG No 7373 bound for Littlehampton, and on the right 4VEP No 7725 bound for Streatham Hill carriage sidings. *Colin Marsden*

97
The first 36 4CIG and 18 4BIG units are fitted with a unique electric parking brake system, rendering them as non-standard to the bulk of the fleet. These units are all allocated to Brighton. If these sets are used on the South Western or Eastern Divisions crewing problems can arise, as drivers may well refuse to operate the units if they are not familiar with the equipment. No 7303 descends from the Crystal Palace line at Bromley Junction with empties from Streatham Hill to Brighton on 5 March 1982. *Colin Marsden*

98
On the CD main line between Coulsdon North and Earlswood there are two alternate routes, one passes through Redhill, and the other — the Quarry line — avoids Redhill. Crossing from the down Quarry line to the down Redhill slow line at Earlswood is a 12CIG/BIG/CIG formation working a Victoria-Brighton semi-fast service on 9 March 1982. *Colin Marsden*

99
It is rare for services on the Western or Central sections to operate with a BIG unit leading, and this normally only occurs when last minute stock substitution has to take place. On 18 July 1981 a Victoria-Littlehampton via Quarry service was captured passing Balcombe with BIG No 7051 leading. *Colin Marsden*

100
Between Balcombe and Haywards Heath lays Copyhold Junction, where the branch line to East Grinstead via Horsted Keynes once diverged; the line is now used just for a short distance to a stone terminal at Ardingly. With branch track disappearing off to the right BIG No 7048 approaches the junction while forming the leading portion of a Victoria-Brighton fast service on 9 March 1982. *Colin Marsden*

101
The Central Division has two main southbound arterial routes, the primary route from Victoria is via East Croydon and Haywards Heath to the south coast, with the secondary route via Epsom, Dorking and Horsham, serving the West Sussex resorts. With some pleasant Sussex scenery in the background a morning Bognor Regis-Victoria train approaches Horsham headed by 4BIG No 7044 on 16 April 1981. *Colin Marsden*

102
Services from Victoria to Eastbourne traverse the Brighton main line as far as Keymer Junction, south of Wivelsfield, from where they go cross-country to Lewes and join the Brighton-Ore Coastway line for the remainder of their journey to Eastbourne. A 12CIG formation passes Wivelsfield station and slows for the junction points at Keymer Junction on 9 March 1982 while working the 13.53 service from Victoria. *Colin Marsden*

103
An afternoon Littlehampton-Victoria via Hove service departs from the northern end of the 1 mile 499yd long Clayton Tunnel situated between Preston Park and Hassocks on the Brighton main line, led by CIG No 7330 on 28 April 1982. Note the guard's periscope lookouts on the roof of the MBSO vehicle. *Colin Marsden*

104
When the first 36 CIG and 18 BIG units were introduced during the mid-1960s they were the first of the 1963 designed units and in many ways the design prototype of future main line stock. One unique feature of these units was the design of the dual air brake/main reservoir isolating cock with its operating handle flush to the front when in the closed position, and at a 45° angle when open. This arrangement was reversed on subsequent units of similar design. *British Railways*

105
The direct route for Littlehampton-Victoria trains is via the Mid-Sussex line and Horsham, however several are routed along the Coastway to Hove and thence via the direct Brighton line to London. A 12CIG formation led by unit No 7388 departs from West Worthing under clear signals during the summer of 1981 with a Littlehampton-Victoria train. *John Vaughan*

106
The CIG/BIG fleet are not allocated to the SED and are therefore rarely seen in that area, however with one of the Region's major repair centres at Chart Leacon (Ashford) units of all types operate to this point at regular intervals. CIG No 7414 is seen here to the south of Pluckley leading two 2HAP units while en route from Stewarts Lane to Chart Leacon. *Colin Marsden*

4VEP

For use on the 1967 electrified Waterloo-Bournemouth line a fleet of high-density four-car corridor units was designed, being based on the previously successful CIG/BIG style units. These new generation outer-suburban/main line units were classified VEP (Vestibule Electro Pneumatic), and in later years classified 423 by BR. The main difference between this fleet and the CIG/BIG series is the high-density styling, ie: more passengers per coach. The actual coach types as used in the CIG sets remained for the VEP build but with major styling differences. On DTC vehicles the first class accommodation was positioned at the opposite end to the driving cab in four compartments with a side corridor; the second class accommodation was in a four bay saloon laid out in the 3+2 seating mode. Unlike the CIG/BIG builds the two DTC vehicles on the VEP units were identical. The TS vehicles were set out in 10 bays, the outer ones of which seat eight passengers while the remaining eight bays seat 10, doors being provided in each seating bay. After the CIG stock entered traffic it was found that the luggage accommodation was insufficient, so on the VEP stock a larger van was positioned in the MBS vehicle, and this, together with the small guard's office takes up nearly half the vehicle length, the remaining area being occupied by six bays in a saloon. Power equipment is carried on the two bogies under the MBS vehicle in the form of 4×250hp English Electric traction motors, two on each bogie, with other power and control equipment carried between the bogies. The first orders for VEP stock were placed during 1965/6 for a batch of 20 units. The first unit carrying running number 7701 emerged during early 1967 with all 20 being on the region and commissioned for service before the introduction of the new Waterloo-Bournemouth electric service in July. As the modernised Waterloo-Bournemouth route was equipped with Automatic Warning System (AWS)

107
Based on the proven CIG/BIG design, the purpose built high-density stock for the newly electrified Waterloo-Bournemouth line commenced delivery to the SR from York during early 1967. Although mechanically based on the CIG/BIG units the VEP stock were internally different with the first class compartments at the opposite end of the DTC than on earlier designs. VEP No 7707 stands in Clapham Junction Yard when on delivery from York. Note the shoe gear is missing. *S. W. Stevens-Stratten*

the first 20 units were built with Westinghouse AWS equipment, whereas subsequent builds did not include this equipment, however most units have more recently been fitted with AWS as track equipment has been progressively installed throughout the region. Prior to the delivery of the first VEP unit subsequent orders were already placed, mainly to replace aged SR stock on the Victoria-Brighton line, and during 1967-1970 a total of 95 units were delivered. One detail difference worth mentioning is that the first 55 units were constructed with lifting lugs protruding from the body line at bogie centre position at frame height. After unit No 7755 these lugs were omitted and lifting had to be carried out with jacks placed directly on to the coach frame. During the early 1970s a further batch of identical units was ordered which were delivered during 1972 carrying running numbers 7816-7853, these were destined to replace many BIL, HAL and COR units from the South Western and Central Divisions.

In 1973 the final order for 4VEP units was placed, this time for 41 units allocated numbers 7854-7894, these were to operate on the South Eastern section to replace some of the two-car outer suburban HAP units, which in turn replaced SUB stock scheduled for withdrawal on the Central and Western Divisions. The VEP stock was constructed at York Works except the TS and MBS cars of the first 20 units that were assembled at Derby Litchurch Lane Carriage Works. When completed units were tested at York and then transferred via Temple Mills to the Southern Region at Selhurst where extensive pre-service testing was carried out, including empty runs to and from Brighton. The livery applied to units when introduced was BR standard blue with small yellow warning panels in the Pullman end door. Full yellow ends appeared after the first 20 units and this practice continued until during 1970 when unit No 7808 was released from York painted in Inter-City livery as a trial for the remainder of the fleet. Following units continued to emerge in all blue until early 1971 when blue-grey livery was adopted as a standard finish throughout BR, earlier all blue units being repainted when receiving classified overhauls. Unit allocations have remained fairly constant throughout their lives with sets allocated to Wimbledon, Bournemouth and Fratton on the SWD, Brighton on the CD and Ramsgate on the SED.

The VEP fleet remained basically intact until 1978 when 12 units Nos 7788-7799 were reclassified as 4VEG (Vestibule Electro Gatwick) and classified 427 by the Southern. These unit had selected seats removed and replaced by luggage racks for use on the Victoria-Gatwick Airport service, this conversion reducing the seating in the second class by 24 to 208. From the outside these units can be identified by the Rail-Air sign applied to the body side, and a continuous Victoria-Gatwick slogan applied at cant rail height. Technical detail and coach types are the same as in VEP stock. It is understood that when the full push-pull Victoria-Gatwick service is instigated during the mid-1980s the VEG units will return to their VEP status. From 1983 some VEG units have passed through works and emerged in standard livery, with no special route insignia.

108
Although the stock was comparative with earlier 1963 builds, testing and training had to take place with a considerable emphasis on driver training as most men who would be working these units on the Bournemouth electrification had not been trained on electric traction previously. Set No 7703 painted in all blue livery with small yellow warning panel, passes Pirbright Junction on 12 June 1967 when on a training run from Basingstoke to Wimbledon. *British Railways*

109
Construction of the VEP fleet continued from the pilot order for 20 units and during 1968 sets were being delivered at the rate of one per week. No 7756 stands in Lancing carriage sidings during 1968 beside the former LB&SCR carriage works. The unit is photographed awaiting acceptance and when this picture was taken the third rail collector shoes had still to be fitted. *John Vaughan*

110
One problem when building stock at York was transportation to the SR. Units could not be driven as no third-rail connection was available, therefore during 1967/9 units were hauled by the ER as far as Doncaster from where a Southern locomotive would collect the stock. Slim-line Class 33 No D6594 passes Knebworth on 9 April 1968 hauling new units Nos 7748/45/47. *D. L Percival*

111
Units delivered prior to 1971 were outshopped in all blue livery with body side numbers applied in white. A 12VEP formation with unit No 7788 leading traverses the Quarry line at Merstham during June 1971 while working a Victoria-Brighton semi-fast service. *Stan Creer*

112
Inter-City blue-grey livery was applied to the VEP fleet from 1971 and all blue units already in service were repainted in dual livery when they next received classified overhaul. After quite a heavy snowfall — in south of England terms — VEP No 7737 passes under West London signalbox on 9 January 1981 while working a Twickenham-Waterloo via Hounslow service. *Colin Marsden*

113

After the various orders for the VEP fleet had been delivered a total of 194 units were in traffic at the end of 1974, although three units had been disbanded to form the VAB unit. The fleet was allocated to, and operated on, all three divisions of the region. Set No 7848 approaches Wimbledon with a down Waterloo-Portsmouth semi-fast service while an eight-car formation of VEP stock passes by in the up direction with an Alton-Waterloo train on 25 August 1980. *Colin Marsden*

114

Units operating on the South Western Division are allocated to Wimbledon (WD), Fratton (FR) and Bournemouth (BM), and at the end of 1982 a total of 88 units were maintained on the division. Passing some 'wet patches' on the up main line, VEP No 7746 approaches New Malden on 12 April 1980 with the 15.01 Waterloo-Guildford via Cobham service. *Colin Marsden*

115
On the SWD the fleet is used in conjunction with CIG stock on outer suburban and main lines, providing a fleet of units capable of operating almost any service. Approaching Surbiton an 8VEP formation led by unit No 7745 slows for the station stop with an Alton/Basingstoke-Waterloo stopping service on 2 February 1980. *Colin Marsden*

116
Passenger accommodation on the VEP units is slightly more cramped than on the CIG fleet, with 48 first and 232 second on the VEP, compared to 42 first and 192 second on the CIG. A rush-hour Waterloo-Portsmouth Harbour service formed of a VEP leading two CIGs passes Walton-on-Thames during the summer of 1980. *Colin Marsden*

117
From their introduction until the mid-1980s all VEP units had curtains in both first and second class vehicles, breaking up the rather plain interior. However due to financial cutbacks when the second class area curtains were scheduled for cleaning, both curtains and body clips were removed. A Waterloo-Basingstoke/Alton semi-fast service passes through West Byfleet station on 15 April 1980. *Colin Marsden*

118
The Waterloo-Bournemouth stopping trains are the services for which the initial fleet of 20 units were built and these are still operated by the VEP fleet. The service from Waterloo is half-hourly with one train per hour terminating at Basingstoke. Up and down Waterloo-Basingstoke stopping services pass to the south of Pirbright Junction on a sunny spring day in 1981. *Colin Marsden*

119
Carrying the Waterloo-Bournemouth stopping headcode '93' VEP No 7847 passes near Wallers Ash with the 11.42 Waterloo-Bournemouth on 5 September 1979. Stopping services from Waterloo take 2hr 4min for the 108-mile journey with 26 intermediate stops. *Colin Marsden*

120
Outer-suburban operations have always featured largely with the VEP fleet and this is more obvious on the Western section. Set No 7817 stops at Bentley on 27 September 1977 while working the 10.40 Alton-Waterloo. The Alton line, which is a branch from the Bournemouth main line diverging at Pirbright, is served by portions of the Waterloo-Bournemouth stopping services. *Colin Marsden*

121
The station buildings at Holmwood have so far escaped modernisation and the pleasant Surrey country station still retains its LB&SCR image. During peak periods some semi-fast services from Victoria to the Sussex Coast are routed by way of Dorking and Horsham and thence the Mid-Sussex line. VEP No 7873 enters the station with a Victoria-Bognor Regis train. *John Vaughan*

122
To augment the SED's substantial fleet of Class 411 (CEP) units some VEPs have been allocated to Ramsgate (RE). The 16.26 Victoria-Ashford via Maidstone service pulls into Charing station, and past the signalbox, formed of VEP No 7780 leading a 2HAP unit on 3 June 1982.
Colin Marsden

123
The hourly stopping trains from Charing Cross to Margate split at Ashford, with the front portion travelling via Dover, and the rear section via Deal and Ramsgate. These services are often formed of VEP stock and here we see the 10.30 service from Charing Cross near Ashford on 15 May 1980. On the rear of the train are two 2HAPs. *Colin Marsden*

124
Victoria-Ramsgate services via Herne Hill, which serve the North Kent towns, are also frequent users of VEP stock. Services on this route are half-hourly and take 2hr 17min for the 79¼ miles. On 2 April 1979 set No 7874 is seen departing from Rainham with the 11.15 service from Victoria. *Colin Marsden*

125
As mentioned in the section introductory text the fleet of VEPs Nos 7788-7799 were converted during 1979 for use on the interim Victoria-Gatwick Airport service. Units have special luggage accommodation fitted in place of some seating, and the legend 'Railair City Link — Gatwick — London' added on the DTC vehicles, in addition to the same wording placed as a band at cant-rail height. After conversion units were reclassified as VEG (Vestibule-Electro-Gatwick) and renumbered. Set No 7912 approaches Clapham Junction on 2 December 1980. *Brian Morrison*

126
All VEG units are allocated to Brighton (BI) and are usually only used on the Gatwick Airport services, but they have been seen working suburban services from Waterloo and even the Wimbledon-Sutton local service. However on 18 May 1982 set No 7905 was operating on the correct route and is seen here departing from Gatwick Airport with the 17.36 Bognor-Victoria service. *Brian Morrison*

VAB

Three units of the 4VEP fleet Nos 7739/41/42 when delivered to Selhurst in 1968 did not take up service in their intended form, and due to a shortage of main line buffet units for the Waterloo-Bournemouth line were formed into a special eight-car buffet unit classified as 8VAB and numbered 8001. The unit contained three power cars Nos 62200/2/3 and four DTCs Nos 76373-6, together with converted buffet car No 1759 modified to EMU requirements. The formation was thus: DTC, MBS, DTC, DTC, MBS, TRB, MBS, DTC. The reason for forming the unit of four DTC vehicles instead of two DTC and two TS was the need for a high proportion of first class accommodation. Being so formed it was possible for a three-car unit and a four-car unit of the same set to be in traffic at the same time, both carrying running number 8001, as these were applied to the cab ends of all DTC vehicles. Minor alterations were carried out to some vehicles in the formation mainly the redesign of MBS No 62203, where saloon accommodation was adjacent to the buffet vehicle, here the 3+2 seating was remodelled as 2+1 with the provision of tables at the majority of bays. Total seating throughout the eight car unit was for 96 first and 299 second class passengers together with 23 in the buffet car. The total weight of the unit was 323 tons and the maximum traction power available was 3,000hp. The 8VAB unit took up operation during mid-1968 and was allocated to Bournemouth. The unit was used quite extensively when first introduced, but as time progressed it became the 'spare' unit more and more often, and when delivery of further REP units took place during 1974 the VAB was disbanded, with most cars being formed back into 4VEP units. When in traffic the VAB could always be recognised some distance away as the VEP cars were painted in standard rail blue livery while the buffet vehicle carried Inter-City livery.

127
Perhaps the most unique of all modern emus was the formation of the VAB during 1968 to assist with powered units on the newly electrified Waterloo-Bournemouth line. The set, formed of VEP emu cars and a loco-hauled buffet car was divided into a three- and five-car formation for operational purposes, and in normal circumstances were not permitted to operate individually. With the three-car set leading No 8001 approaches Vauxhall with a Bournemouth-Waterloo semi-fast on 10 July 1970. *John Faulkner*

128
It was very unusual to find the VAB formation working anywhere but the Bournemouth line, so this illustration of the unit working with a Class 33 away from the third-rail system at Romsey is very rare. The diversion from the main line was due to engineering work. The route between Southampton and Eastleigh via Romsey has clearance passed for third-rail fitted stock, without the need for the pickup shoes to be lifted. *John Bird*

129
The VAB unit usually operated with the three-car 'set' at the London end of the formation, shown here as the train passes West Byfleet, still with semaphore signalling in use on 24 February 1970. Normally the VAB unit would be kept spare at Bournemouth only being used when there was an acute shortage of other suitable stock. *John Scrace*

REP/TC

With the introduction of electric services on the Waterloo-Bournemouth line from 1967 new electric stock was required, but as the line continuing on from Bournemouth to Weymouth was not to be electrified, a major problem presented itself to the SR Board, to design a traction that could operate on the electrified system to Bournemouth, and then be either self-propelled or locomotive hauled to and from Weymouth. Also the short section of line between Southampton and the Docks could not be forgotten, and again despite no electrification being carried out, the new generation of units being built would be required to operate over these lines. After much local and Board deliberations it was decided to use four-coach formations, some of which would be powered, while the majority or others would be trailer sets provided with a driving position at each end. Such was the success of the SR push-pull experiments during the early 1960s that they knew that a 'high powered' tractor was quite capable of propelling up to eight cars at speeds of 90mph and above quite successfully. It was planned that each train required to operate between Waterloo and Bournemouth/Weymouth would be formed of one high powered 'tractor' unit (4REP) formed at the London end of the train which would propel one or two trailer control (TC) sets. After arrival at Bournemouth the 'tractor' unit would be detached and the trailer portion hauled on to Weymouth by one of the Region's push-pull fitted Class 33/1 locomotives. From Weymouth the stock would be propelled back to Bournemouth being driven from the remote cab of the trailer unit, taking power and control from the Class 33. On arrival at Bournemouth the train would be recoupled to the 'tractor' unit and the locomotive detached from the back, enabling the formation to proceed to Waterloo with the electric 'tractor' unit providing the power.

For this new service a substantial fleet of new stock was required. One basic criteria the SR had to bear in mind was their long term intention to be able to couple any of the Region's modern stock together for multiple-unit operation, so when the new generation Bournemouth line stock was built it closely resembled the previously constructed CIG/BIG and VEP units in body styling, but the technical specification was totally different. As the new stock would be required to haul and propel other units much higher power than on previous emu trains would be required, therefore it was decided to revert to the older practice of having the power cars at the end of the formation but to retain the centre guard's position, thus being the first break from Southern tradition of having the guard's accommodation in the powered vehicle. For this new service a fleet of 11 high powered 'tractor' units were ordered and classified as 4REP by the SR. In later days they became Class 430 and BR numbering was in the 30xx range. The driving cars were identical at both ends of the unit and were classified as DMS (Driving Motor Second). The cab was of the same design as used on the CIG/BIG/VEP builds but slightly larger; behind this was a full width vestibule for cab access. The passenger accommodation was divided into two saloons of four bays separated by a centre vestibule with seating arranged in the low-density 2+2 style, at the inner end of the coach a full width passenger vestibule was provided. The power equipment situated under this coach consisted of half the train's power system, provided by four 400hp English Electric traction motors, one mounted on each axle, thus giving a total train power of 3,200hp, and giving the sets the distinction of being the most powerful emu train in operation in the country at the time of their introduction. Due to the high power of these units a 'load limit' is imposed where a REP with all its motors operable must not work in multiple with any other powered unit except a MLV or single two-car unit, otherwise overloading of the sub-station would occur. A mass of electrical equipment is carried between the two powered bogies. Nose end connections of the driving cars are the same as on other units of similar design, except that an electric train heating power jumper cable is carried under the driver's side buffer. Between the two powered vehicles is situated a TRB (Trailer Restaurant Buffet) and TBF (Trailer Brake First). The TRB cars were rebuilt from 1961 BRCW built RBs the first being dealt with at Eastleigh, while the remainder were modernised to emu standards at York. During rebuilding little alteration to the internal layout was carried out and in their new form sat 23 unclassified passengers in the 2+1 mode, however alterations were made to the cooking facilities and surrounding area where all equipment was converted to electric operation and two toilets added adjacent to the kitchen for staff use. External doors were sealed up except for goods loading and emergency exits. When introduced on to the Bournemouth line buffet cars were named, mainly after places to which the units travelled but there were some odd choices:

Unit No	*Buffet Car No*	*Buffet name (carried inside coach)*
3001	69319	*The Kingston*
3002	69320	*The Waterloo*
3003	69321	*The Farnborough*
3004	69322	*The Solent*
3005	69323	*The Hampton Court*
3006	69324	*The Bournemouth*
3007	69325	*The Winchester*
3008	69326	*The Sandown*
3009	69327	*The Wimbledon*
3010	69328	*The Vauxhall*
3011	69329	*The Beaulieu*
3012*	69022	*The Brooklands*
3013*	69023	*The Avon*
3014*	69024	*The New Forest*
3015*	69025	*The Stour*

*1974/5 built

The TBF vehicle of the formation was again rebuilt from a standard Mk 1 coach and for this a fleet of CK (Composite Corridor) coaches were used with heavy alterations. This work included the removal of the second class accommodation and fitting a brake van and small guard's office in its space, re-detailing the first class compartments, modernising the lavatories, and fitting air/EP brake equipment. Although the fleet of 11 REP units operated the service very well with the trailer control sets, there was little margin for extended maintenance or failure of the units, and this together with improvement of the service in the 1970s required more units. During 1973 a further four 4REP units were ordered identical in design to the previous fleet and delivered during 1974/5, all being built at York Works. Again the DMS cars were built from new but the TRB and TBF vehicles were rebuilt from salvaged locomotive hauled stock. As the driving cars of these units were built new to Mk 1 coach profile as late as 1975 these must be the last Mk I coaches built and it is interesting to note that Mk III loco-hauled vehicles were under construction at the same time. One difference with the 1974/5 build units was with the buffet car. These were rebuilt from former RU vehicles and sport a different external window arrangement to the earlier type. When introduced the original 11 units were painted in all blue livery, which subsequently changed to blue/grey during the early 1970s. However, 1974/5 units emerged in blue/grey livery from new.

To operate with this fleet of high powered 'tractor' units a fleet of TC (Trailer Control) sets in three and four car formations were built, entirely formed of rebuilt and modernised loco hauled stock of various types. The formation of each series was thus: 3TC: DTS, TBS, DTS. 4TC: DTS, TBS, TFK, DTS. A total of three 3TC units and 28 4TCs were built. In body appearance these TC units closely followed the REP design but of course, the one fundamental difference was the omission of power equipment and thus these units always had to be in multiple with a power

130
Deemed by many as the 'Deltics' of the Southern, the REP fleet with their 3,200hp are the most powerful electric units in operation in the country, except of course, the APT! A Bournemouth-Waterloo service passes Beaulieu Road with the pioneer REP No 3001 leading and a TC unit.
John Vaughan

source. The DTS car had the same internal layout to the DMS of the REP fleet and these were rebuilt from TSO vehicles, with two former toilets being rebuilt as the driver's cab and adjoining vestibule. Eastleigh Works undertook the first rebuilding but all subsequent work was undertaken by York. The TBS (Trailer Brake Second) vehicles were rebuilt from BSK coaches and during this work the basic formation remained but the complete coach was modernised to the latest style, again the first vehicle of the type was rebuilt at Eastleigh Works and the remainder dealt with at York. The TFK (Trailer First Corridor) vehicles were rebuilt from loco hauled FK coaches with modernisation to the latest standards. This was carried out at York except for the prototype vehicle rebuilt at Eastleigh. The numbering allocated to the TCs was 301-303 for three-car formations and 401-428 for the four-car formations. The main reason for forming the three-car sets was that when a train was formed of one 3TC and two 4TC sets and a locomotive, it would only take up the same platform space as a 12 car emu formation. This was particularly important at Waterloo, for few platforms were able to deal with more than a 12-car train. Another use for the units was to be on the Southampton Docks boat trains, where a three-car formation was to be formed on the rear of a regular service train and detached at Southampton Central for the short journey to the Docks. However this was seldom the case and these three units were more often seen in general formation on the Waterloo-Bournemouth line giving rise to passenger congestion during the summer months. The total passenger accommodation of a 3TC was 160 second class passengers, and a 4TC 42 first and 160 second class, the total weight of a three-car unit being 99 tonnes and a four-car 132 tonnes. With delivery of the four further REP units during 1974/5 it was decided to augment the 3TC formations to four-coaches by converting a further fleet of TFK cars. Again these rebuilds were undertaken from the loco hauled FK fleet at York Works. When reformed into four-cars, units were renumbered in the 4TC range and became 429-431. At the same time three 'new' 4TC units were converted at York, in the same manner as the 1966 builds, and these became 432-434, and were identical to the earlier build. The livery applied to units built during 1966/7 was all blue, this changed from 1971 to blue and grey. Sets introduced during the 1970s were however built in blue/grey livery. From new, all the REP and TC units have been allocated to Bournemouth Depot (BM) where all maintenance is carried out, extended overhauls being dealt with at Chart Leacon, and major shopping being undertaken at Eastleigh BREL Works. The REP/TC fleet is often referred to in railway operating circles as 1966 stock. One of the advantages of the TC fleet being able to operate in multiple with the Class 33/1 or 73 locomotives, is that during recent years it has been regular operating practice to use these units and a locomotive in other areas away from the Waterloo-Bournemouth line, and have worked on Clapham Junction-Kensington Olympia, Waterloo-Salisbury and Reading-Portsmouth routes.

131
The REP tractor fleet were built at York works with DMS vehicles being of new build and intermediate trailers converted from loco-hauled Mk 1 stock. When introduced the first 11 units were outshopped in all blue livery with small yellow warning panel, but after a short period on the SR this was changed to the standard Inter-City colours. DMS No S62148 of unit No 3004 stands outside York works on one of the traversers during early 1967. *Author's Collection*

132
The buffet cars for the REP fleet were converted from loco-hauled RB vehicles originally built during 1961 by BRCW Ltd. This view shows the interior of the new TRB (Trailer Restaurant Buffet) vehicle from the accommodation end. Bar counter and cooking facilities are at the far end.
Author's Collection

133
Although all vehicles of the TC fleets were rebuilt from former loco-hauled stock, none of the old internal layout remained in these 'new' trains. The upper view shows the interior of a first class compartment in the TF (Trailer First) vehicle showing modern seat styles and upholstery with aluminium luggage racks above, a wall mirror and two reading lights provided each side. In the lower view the interior of a second class compartment in the TBS (Trailer Brake Second) is shown, converted from a BSK with four seats provided each side and a large aluminium luggage rack above and wall mounted reading lights. *British Railways*

134
Body styling of the REP/TC fleet closely followed the CIG/VEP designs but units are recognisable from the front end, as the REP/TC fleet have a train heating jumper below the driver's side buffer. While operating a training trip TC No 402 travels through the New Forest early in 1967. In this view the buck-eye coupling is in the lowered position. *GEC Traction Ltd*

135
Although the formation of the three 3TC units was intended as an advantage, from an operational view they were of little assistance and during 1974 were augmented into four-car units by the addition of a TF. Coupled to a non push-pull fitted Class 33, 3TC No 302 stands at Eastleigh on 18 May 1968. *C. H. S. Owen*

136
Due to the late delivery of some vehicles, particularly the TF (Trailer First), some 4TC units arrived on the SR as three-car sets and some saw service in this form. This rare photograph shows two 4TC units operating as three-car sets being propelled by Class 73/1 electro diesel No E6012 at Shawford Junction. The driver would be able to control the locomotive in both electric and diesel mode from the cab of the TC, by means of the 27 wire multi-control system. *Alastair McIntyre*

137
The fleet of 19 Class 33 locomotives fitted for push-pull operation with the new Bournemouth line stock, entered service from the middle of 1967 and their equipment enabled them to be formed any where in a train formation, even in the middle. Sandwiched between two TC units Class 33/1 No D6521 provides the traction power for a Bournemouth-Waterloo train, shown departing from Bournemouth during 1967. *A. Swain*

138
Once the SR had taken delivery of its fleet of TC stock and push-pull fitted Class 33 and 73 locomotives, weird and wonderful formations were recorded. Approaching Basingstoke with a fast service from Bournemouth to Waterloo, a 12TC formation receives its traction power from two 1,600hp electro-diesels marshalled in the centre of the formation. *John Faulkner*

139
Soon after the introduction of modernised Waterloo-Bournemouth/Weymouth line services from the summer of 1967, the SR Board could see that operationally the service was going to be a success. The fleet of 19 push-pull fitted Class 33 locomotives were completed in time for the service introduction in April 1967. No D6536 carrying cab mounted multiple-unit jumpers hauls a TC unit to the west of Bournemouth with the front portion of the 10.30 Waterloo-Weymouth on 8 July 1967. *British Railways*

140
Such is the design of REP/TC stock that it is possible for various trailer vehicles to be cross marshalled and this is most common when a TC unit is loaned the buffet car from a REP set, usually for Royal Train operations. On 1 August 1979 when HM Queen Elizabeth the Queen Mother travelled from Portsmouth Harbour to Waterloo, TC No 416 was remarshalled with the TRB and TBF of a REP, and hauled by Class 73 No 73.142. The train is seen here at Waterloo after arrival. *Colin Marsden*

141
REP units are usually marshalled at the London end of a train because of operational reasons at Bournemouth where the unit is detached from Weymouth line services, thus propelling its 8TC load in a south-westerly direction. REP No 3006 passes Wimbledon West on 17 March 1981 while heading a semi-fast Bournemouth-Waterloo service.
Colin Marsden

142
Although when the REP is marshalled on the rear of a formation it is propelling some 264 tons of TC unit, little snatching occurs between the vehicles, mainly attributable to the design of the buck-eye couplings between vehicles and the skill of the drivers who operate the trains. On 12 April 1980 the 14.46 Waterloo-Bournemouth travels between Raynes Park and New Malden led by TC No 425.
Colin Marsden

143
Due to the large amount of power taken from the third-rail by a REP tractor unit it is not possible to operate two units in multiple. For multiple operation a REP is only permitted to operate with a single MLV, or a two-car unit. However if two REPs are required to operate between depots, the motors on one unit would be isolated, as was the case on 12 July 1979 when units Nos 3005/9 worked from Chart Leacon to Bournemouth, seen here passing Surbiton. *Colin Marsden*

144
It is very rare for REP units to work over any section of line other than that between Waterloo and Bournemouth, and since their introduction in 1967 the majority of units have clocked up well over two million miles. Probably travelling at the line speed of 90mph REP No 3006 leads the usual 8TC formation under Hampton Court Junction flyover with a semi-fast service from Bournemouth to Waterloo on 26 August 1980. *Colin Marsden*

145
The fast services on the Waterloo-Bournemouth line take 1hr 36min for the 108 mile journey with one intermediate stop at Southampton for one minute. The 08.41 Bournemouth (07.32 Weymouth) traverses the up main line approaching West Byfleet on 8 April 1980, led by REP No 3006. It is usual practice to operate the REPs so that their buffet vehicle is second from the front. *Colin Marsden*

146
Fast services from Waterloo to Bournemouth depart at 00.35min past each hour and provided they have a clear run, can pass Woking at 90mph within 24min of leaving the capital. TC No 402 hurries the 11.35 service from Waterloo past Woking Junction. In the background is one of the SWD permanent way depots. *Colin Marsden*

147
When initially converted the REP/TC fleet were planned for 100mph operation but as time has proved the SR line speed has remained at 90, and with financial cutbacks the required track maintenance to increase the speed is unlikely to be authorised. Passing Pirbright Junction TC No 415 leads the 14.46 Waterloo-Bournemouth semi-fast on 15 April 1980. *Colin Marsden*

148
The total passenger loading of a 12-car REP/TC formation is 579 made up of 448 second and 108 first class, with 23 unclassified seats in the dining car. REP No 3010 leads an early morning semi-fast Bournemouth-Waterloo service out of St Johns cutting and towards Woking on 9 April 1981. *Colin Marsden*

149
The push-pull system between Bournemouth and Weymouth operated by a Class 33/1 and a TC unit proved highly successful, therefore during the late 1970s the system was adopted for other routes, in particular on the Reading-Portsmouth, and Waterloo-Salisbury line. TC No 416 stops at Mortimer while forming a Reading-Portsmouth service on 28 May 1978. When operating on this route the Class 33/1 is usually kept at the Portsmouth end of the formation. *Colin Marsden*

150
The Waterloo-Bournemouth semi-fast service depart from Waterloo at 00.45min past each hour, and stop at Woking, Basingstoke, Winchester, Eastleigh, Southampton Airport, Southampton, Brockenhurst, New Milton and Christchurch, covering the 108 miles in 2hr 6min. TC No 414 approaches Winchester and passes the 'Baltic' siding on 7 July 1981 with the 10.45 service from Waterloo. *Colin Marsden*

151
All the REP/TC fleet is allocated to Bournemouth (BM) depot which undertakes general maintenance. Classified overhauls are carried out at Chart Leacon (Ashford, Kent) and major overhauls at Eastleigh BREL works. An up country semi-fast service passes Class 47 No 47.345 in Bevois Park yard during July 1981, headed by REP No 3003. *Colin Marsden*

152
Surprisingly few stations on the Waterloo-Bournemouth line have been reduced to 'bus shelter' accommodation and station buildings on both sides of the line are still retained at Christchurch with wooden platform buildings and a covered station footbridge. Awaiting departure from the station on 13 April 1982 is the 17.02 Bournemouth-Waterloo led by REP No 3007. *Colin Marsden*

4VEC/3TIS

One of the most unique lines in the BR network is the section between Ryde Pier Head and Shanklin on the Isle of Wight. Back in 1965 the line and its equipment was up for early replacement but as the Southern's finances were at a low ebb, complete closure of the remaining system between Ryde and Ventnor, and Ryde and Newport/Cowes were rumoured. Under the Beeching axe it was publicly announced that it was the BTCs intention to close both lines, but such was the public outcry at these intended closures that a public enquiry was held by the TUCC, under the auspices of the MOT. The eventual outcome was that the section of line between Ryde and Newport/Cowes was to be completely closed and replaced by road transport. BR was now faced with the decision of what to do regarding motive power and stock for the line as due to the Island's restricted loading gauge it was impossible for mainland stock to be used. During mid-1965 the London Transport Executive (LTE) had a surplus of 1920s built tube stock from the Northern City line, and rather than build any new stock BR purchased this secondhand power for use on the Island. Initially when BR viewed the stock prior to purchase it was their intention to convert it to diesel operation, using conventional Gardner bus engines, but it was subsequently decided that the line could be operated more effectively if it was electrified. Electrification was soon authorised and commenced during January 1966 being completed within 15 months. Following withdrawal from LTE use the stock was taken to their works at Acton where a full mechanical and electrical overhaul took place including the conversion of the stock from four- to three-rail operation. A total of 42 coaches was required to operate the new railway but something nearer 55 cars were purchased by BR as better vehicles became available after the initial purchase. The extra vehicles were used to supply spare components which were stripped on the mainland and stored, the vehicle bodies going for scrap. Once the 42 vehicles that were to be used had been completed at Acton they were hauled to Wimbledon by LTE battery locomotives from where they operated under their own power to Stewarts Lane depot for painting and various internal modifications. Once completed and tested to BR requirements, units were 'run-in' between Wimbledon and Woking and on the Portsmouth line, making a rare sight of underground profile stock operating on the BR main line system. As the new stock would be required to take up passenger service only shortly after its arrival on the Island, crew training was carried out in conjunction with running-in on the mainland. Vehicles were all constructed on steel underframes with timber body framing and steel outer panelling. Originally cars were built by various companies ie: Union Construction Company, Metropolitan Carriage & Wagon Company and Cammel Laird between 1923 and 1934. For use on the Island, trains of two different formations were marshalled, six three-car sets (3TIS) and six four-car sets (4VEC) later classified by BR as Class 486 and 485 respectively. Numbering of the units were: 3TIS — 031-036; 4VEC — 041-046 (VEC and TIS was derived from the Roman name for the Isle of Wight — 'Vectis').

The 3TIS formations being MBSO (Motor Brake Second Open), TSO (Trailer Second Open), DTSO (Driving Trailer Second Open), while 4VEC sets were formed MBSO (Motor Brake Second Open), TSO (Trailer Second Open), DTSO (Driving Trailer Second Open), MBSO (Motor Brake Second Open). The intermediate DTSO car of the 4VEC sets being a non-operable driving vehicle. In the MBSO vehicle an equipment compartment is carried directly behind the driving cab containing most of the traction equipment. Passenger accommodation being provided for 26. On these cars one double and one single leaf sliding door was provided on each side. TSO vehicles were laid out for 42 passengers and in these cars two sets of double leaf sliding doors were provided on each side. On DTSO cars the driving cab is only small, with no major equipment carried, passenger accommodation provided for 38, with two sets of double leaf sliding doors on each side of the coach. The total seating on a 3TIS being 106 and a 4VEC 132. Of course in actual practice far more passengers are able to stand and up to three times this number could easily be carried. During the conversion work at Stewarts Lane some seats were removed and replaced by luggage racks. Power equipment is carried under the MBSO car in the form of two 240hp Metropolitan Vickers traction motors. Late in 1966 when the stock was completed on the mainland vehicles were gathered at Fratton from where they were taken from the track and mounted on Pickfords low loaders for their journey to the Island via the Portsmouth-Fishbourne car ferry. Once on the Island they were railed at Ryde St Johns Road Depot. After initial 'on Island' testing the units commenced passenger operation on 20 March 1967. The livery applied to units when converted was BR standard blue, with full yellow warning ends, and these units hold the distinction of being the first SR emus to be so treated. During 1982 when it was quite obvious that no 'new' stock would be made available for the line in the foreseeable future, a 'light' refurbishing scheme was undertaken with units returning to traffic painted in Inter-City livery and having seating reupholstered.

For technical reasons units can only operate formed in one direction and each driving vehicle is labelled either A or D. 'A' cars always facing Ryde and 'D' vehicles always facing Shanklin. There is only one depot on the Network at Ryde St Johns Road, here all depot and routine maintenance is carried out, always to a very high standard.

It was usual from 1967 until mid-1980 for unit formations to remain constant and trains to operate formed of like numbered pairs ie: 031+041, but following refurbishing repairs when some cars were deemed as uneconomic to repair, reformations have taken place, but trains only ever operate in 3, 4 or 7-car formations.

153
After BR purchased the redundant LTE 1927 tube stock for the Isle of Wight system minor modifications were carried out at LTs works at Acton, before the stock could be handed over at Wimbledon, where the stock was brought by LT via the District Line. Preparation for its new roll took place at Stewarts Lane. On 11 June 1966 a three-car formation stripped of its LT red livery, stands at Wimbledon awaiting transfer to the SR. *John Faulkner*

154
After the necessary preparation work had been undertaken and the stock repainted in BR livery, tests and crew training took place on the mainland prior to shipping to the Isle of Wight, and during the early part of 1967 became a regular sight between Wimbledon Park and Woking. This rear three-quarter view of VEC No 045 was taken at Weybridge during February 1967 when the stock was returning to Wimbledon during a crew training trip. *K. P. Lawrence*

155
The transportation of the stock to the Isle of Wight was quite a spectacle with each car individually loaded on to a Pickfords low-loader and taken by road to Portsmouth, from where they travelled on board the Fishbourne bound car ferry. The first coach to be transferred was car No S38 and is seen here being manipulated on to the deck of the *Camber Queen* at Portsmouth on 2 September 1966.
Author's Collection

156
Once on the Isle of Wight the stock was driven through the streets of Ryde on the low-loader to Ryde St Johns Road depot where a special off-loading ramp was prepared. DMBS No S8 is seen here being positioned by the ramp as an Isle of Wight Class 02 tank stands in the adjacent siding. *British Railways*

157/158
Such was the urgency in preparation of the 'new railway' on the Isle of Wight that only two days after arrival of the first vehicle it was hauled around the network by Class 02 0-4-4T No 24 *Calbourne* on 4 September. As the vehicle was not fitted with standard couplings a match wagon was quickly converted and in these two views car No S38 departs from Ryde St Johns Road, and in the lower picture, approaches Sandown. Note the conductor rails laying in the six foot between the two tracks, prior to installation.
Both: Dr J. Mackett

159
Normally Isle of Wight trains operate as seven-car sets, formed of a 3TIS and 4VEC unit, however it is possible for single three of four-car trains to be used, but this is not common practice, except on the Ryde Pier Head-Ryde Esplanade shuttle service, where occasionally a four-car set is to be found. 4VEC No 042 leads 3TIS No 032 out of Brading with the 13.41 Shanklin-Ryde on 13 June 1982.
Colin Marsden

160
During 1982, when it was realised that no new stock would be available for the system for a considerable time, a light refurbishing scheme was authorised. One car at a time was taken into Ryde Works and redecorated inside with new upholstery and a complete repaint. The outsides of the units were also repaired and repainted in modern two-tone blue and grey livery with the legend 'Isle of Wight' applied on the body side. During refurbishment units were also renumbered into the six figure TOPS system. Class 486 No 486.036 leads the 13.21 Shanklin-Ryde into Brading on 13 June 1982. *Colin Marsden*

161
To cover for maintenance or an emergency, the system has one spare motor coach No S10. This car carries a frame in the non-driving side front window, to carry the unit number the vehicle is marshalled in. Whilst the refurbishing programme was underway No S10 was in almost daily use. This car forms the leading vehicle of 3TIS No 031 (running as a four-car unit) in this picture taken at Sandown during the summer of 1982. *Colin Marsden*

162
The formation of units remained constant until 1981/2 but after refurbishment went ahead various 3TIS units operated as four-car sets, with some 4VECs with only three coaches. Passing Smallbrook Junction where the former branch to Newport once diverged, is a fully refurbished seven-car set led by 3TIS No 486.036 forming the 17.21 Shanklin-Ryde on 13 June 1982. *Colin Marsden*

163
Isle of Wight sets carry a letter code on the cab end denoting the correct direction of the car, 'A' cars facing Ryde and 'D' cars Shanklin. This letter is clearly visible above the non-driving window in this view of set No 485.043 departing from Ryde Esplanade with a Shanklin service. The section of line between Ryde Esplanade and Pier Head is worked as two separate single lines, with no points at all on the pier; transfer between up and down lines taking place near Ryde Esplanade. *Colin Marsden*

164
Signalling on the IOW system is a mixture of semaphore and colour light, controlled from three signalboxes at Ryde St Johns Road, Brading and Sandown. Approaching Sandown set No 485.043 slows for the station stop with the 11.55 Ryde-Shanklin on a sunny June day in 1982. In the background some of the Islands departmental stock can be seen, which is normally used only during the winter months. *Colin Marsden*

165
Maintenance of all the Islands stock is carried out at Ryde St Johns, where the depot doubles as a works. In this view set No 485.041 is parked partly in the shed, while to the left a seven-car formation led by set No 032 is stabled, between duties. In the platform set No 485.043 forms a passenger service to Shanklin. On the far right protruding from the old Ryde Works is a withdrawn vehicle awaiting stripping so that any reusable parts may be retained. *Colin Marsden*

166
When a full seven-car formation is in use the total passenger loading is for 238 second class passengers with sufficient room for up to another 150-200 standing. The internal comfort of the stock is not all that it could be, as besides passengers, fish, forklift trucks and metal loading pallets were also conveyed during a visit to the line in 1982. A set formed of VEC 044 and TIS 034 approaches Ryde St Johns Road with the 11.41 Shanklin-Ryde on 14 June 1982. *Colin Marsden*

167
The present network on the Isle of Wight is $8\frac{1}{2}$ miles between Ryde Pier and Shanklin, with intermediate stops at Ryde Esplanade, Ryde St Johns Road, Brading and Sandown; the journey takes 21 minutes with off peak services half-hourly and 20 minutes on Sundays. Four trains are normally required to keep the service running. Resting between duties by modern buffer stops at Shanklin is 3TIS No 032 forming the rear portion of the 10.41 service to Ryde on Sunday, 13 June 1982. *Brian Morrison*

168
Although red electric rear marker lights are provided, red rear discs are often used, as shown here on 3TIS No 486.036 departing from Ryde St Johns Road with a Shanklin bound service. During the 1980s much speculation has been made regarding new stock for the Island but with limited loading restrictions and the economic climate, unless further redundant LTE stock is purchased the future of the line must be in the balance. *Brian Morrison*

PEP

It was during the late 1960s that plans were put forward for a new generation of suburban emu train. At the time various new electrification programmes were in advanced stages of planning and new units would be required to operate them. On the Southern Region vast numbers of new vehicles would be required within the next 10 years to replace ageing SUB units. During 1970 it was decided to build a prototype fleet of three-units, two four-car sets and one two-car set with gangways throughout, which could operate in passenger service as well as undergo testing to evaluate equipment and design, which could be incorporated in forthcoming emu types. All vehicles of the new design were of similar appearance except that some cars had driving positions while others did not. One design feature of the new generation stock announced at an early stage was that each axle of the train would be powered to achieve rapid acceleration, a basic requirement for a busy commuter transit system.

Passenger accommodation was provided in open coaches with seats in the 2+2 style, driving vehicles seating 68, while the intermediate cars in four-car formations accommodated 72, all in the second class mode. Such was the design of the coaches that plenty of standing space for passengers was provided and it was quite possible for twice the number of seated passengers to travel in each unit. The actual coach design was quite new to railway operation in having a basically flat roof, with body side curving outwards from frame height to seat level, then tapering inwards towards roof height, giving maximum use of the permitted loading gauge. The main new innovation to modern coach building was the incorporation of air operated sliding doors in passenger compartments which could either be operated by the guard or the passenger, two sets of doors being provided on each side of driving cars and three on the intermediate vehicles. Unit ends were also of a completely new design with a sloping profile, couplings were also non-standard of the 'Scharfenberg' automatic type, incorporating physical, air and electrical couplings in one movement, operated from controls in the driver's cab. Another change from conventional design was the absence of buffers, all buffing strain being taken by the centre coupling. The driver's cab was of standard design taking up less than half the nose end width. An interesting features was for the first time no guard's van/office was provided, meaning that the guard had to travel in the unoccupied driving cab. Various new designs in power and control equipment were built into the new units, including the use of rheostatic braking in addition to standard EP brakes, for initial 'high speed' de-celeration, and for slow speed stopping EP operated clamp disc brakes were fitted. The heat dissipated during braking being utilised for train heating, which is pressure ventilated throughout the train. When built the sets were fully air conditioned with no opening windows but during trials it was found that more ventilation was required and subsequently sliding top lights were fitted to the main panels prior to the units introduction into traffic. Although each vehicle was a power car, third-rail collector shoes were only provided on the driving vehicles and, on the inner bogies of the intermediate vehicles of four-car sets. The first of the 'new generation' units classified as PEP by the SR was delivered to the Southern from York Works during May 1971. This was a four-car set and carried running number 4001. By the end of that year sister unit No 4002 was delivered and staff and crew training was well underway. During the following year a two-coach unit No 2001 emerged and rather surprisingly it was in unpainted aluminium livery with red bodyside insignia. After training and essential testing had been carried out all three units were put to work normally operating in six- or eight-car formations on the South Western Division on Waterloo-Shepperton, Hampton Court and Chessington duties, other suburban routes not being passed for their operation. The only other routes where these units operated for a short period of one month during 1973 was on the Charing Cross/Cannon Street suburban lines.

During 1972/3 various cars from units were reformed for evaluation of equipment including the reforming on a permanent basis of one of the aluminium cars from set No 2001 into a four-car set. During 1974 the two-car unit was withdrawn from passenger service and converted into a three-car unit for AC/DC power trials as a forerunner to the Class 313 units of ER. After this use the set operated under test conditions in Scotland paving the way for Class 314s but in more recent years has been out of use and in store at Derby.

The two four-car units continued in operation on

the SWD until October 1976 when both were taken out of traffic and stored at East Wimbledon Depot. After some months the units visited Derby Railway Technical Centre for examination and after a further short period passed into departmental stock where they still remain today. During operation of the units passenger reaction was closely monitored and action was taken on production stock derived from the design thus giving passengers the style and design most required.

169
It was the BREL works at York, long associated with emu building, that was given the contract to build the three prototype PEP units and thus the birth of the 1972 design high-density stock. The initial order was placed during 1970 with construction commencing during the middle of that year, continuing until May 1971 when the first four-car unit was ready for despatch to the SR. Set No 4001 still awaiting completion stands inside York carriage works during March 1971. *Author's Collection*

170
During the late 1960s a full sized mock-up of the proposed 'New Generation' suburban electric passenger unit was built at the Railway Technical Centre (RTC) at Derby. In this view the basic shape of the 1972 design can be seen, but the front end was completely redesigned. It is interesting to note that a two position headcode was fitted to this mock-up as well as a wooden facsimile of a 'Scharfenberg' coupling.
British Railways

171
Following delivery of the first unit to the SR during May 1971 it was allocated to Wimbledon Park, from where a staff training programme was initiated so 'on line' testing could begin. The initial testing ground for the unit was on the Alton line, where many thousands of miles were clocked up. Here set No 4001 stands outside Wimbledon Park depot on 18 July 1971. *Author's Collection*

172
Carrying the Waterloo-Waterloo via Hounslow loop headcode, a line the unit did not work over, No 4001 stands at Waterloo during the summer of 1971 for inspection by management and supervisory staff. It will be noted that when the unit was delivered non-opening passenger windows were fitted, these were later replaced by windows with an opening top portion following vehicle ventilation problems during the test programme. *British Railways*

173
Interior of PEP unit: the passenger accommodation in the intermediate vehicles was divided into four bays, separated by the three sets of double leaf sliding doors on each side of the coach. The seats had much lower backs than on previous units, and many complaints were received about their uncomfortable nature from both passengers and the TUCC. It is interesting to note that passenger controlled doors were installed when this illustration was taken, a feature removed prior to the units entering passenger service.
British Railways

174
5 June 1973 was the first day the PEP carried fare paying passengers, when an eight-car formation was put into use on the 10.56/14.26 Waterloo-Hampton Court and 11.43/15.13 return services, thus making the Hampton Court line the first route in Britain to use new generation high density passenger stock. On 1 October 1973 sets Nos 4001/4002 depart from Thames Ditton with the 12.43 Hampton Court-Waterloo service. Note the rear set No 4002 is formed with an aluminium car of set No 2001. *John Scrace*

175
Comparison of the SR's long established commuter trains — the 4SUB and the proposed commuter train of the future. This view was taken at Hampton Court on 24 September 1973, while the PEP units were in passenger service. A team of market researchers often travelled on the train to gauge public opinions and hopefully to gain useful information to improve design to the production trains. *John Scrace.*

176
The two-car unit numbered 2001 was outshopped in 1972 in unpainted aluminium livery with red BR double arrow logo and vehicle numbers. After arrival on SR the unit operated a number of tests between Wimbledon and Alton on its own, before being placed into service with a four-car unit. Here 2PEP No 2001 leads a six-car formation near Wimbledon on a Hampton Court service. *John Faulkner*

177
Following various reformations at Wimbledon Park, which culminated in one of the four-car units receiving an aluminium car, and set No 2001 an all blue vehicle, set No 2001 was taken out of SR service and handed over to the Research and Development section at Derby where an additional trailer was built. The train was then converted for 25kV overhead operation and used as a test bed being renumbered 920.001. The unit is seen here passing Marks Tey on the ER on 14 October 1975. *Malcolm Pudduck*

Class 508

Following extensive testing of the 2 and 4PEP units on the Southern during 1973/5, the basic design for the new generation emu was formed. The first production batch to derive from the SR prototypes were the Class 313 three-car dual voltage units for use on Eastern Region, and the actual production models incorporated many design changes from the original prototype including redesigned flat front ends, modified passenger accommodation, different power equipment and alternative style end couplings. Other production batches were built as follows: Class 314 for the Scottish Region, Class 507 for Midland Region and Class 315 for Eastern Region, but the production batch for the Southern did not emerge until 1979 when the first of a fleet of 43 units classified by BR as 508 and numbered 508.001-508.043 was delivered. Production was carried out at York with units being hauled between match wagons to the Southern via Temple Mills. Four-car units were built for the Southern formed with a DMS (Driving Motor Second) at each end with two TS (Trailer Second) vehicles between. The external appearance resembled PEP stock in many ways, incorporating all open passenger accommodation with passenger controlled sliding doors and no guard's brake or van. The driving cabs in DMS cars take up less than half the width of the end vestibule with a door provided to shut off the actual driving position when not in use, the vestibule being used as the guard's coupe or for passenger accommodation, depending on its position in a train. 74 second class seats are provided in driving vehicles mainly in the 2+3 mode, but some seating near passenger doors is in the 2+2 mode to ease internal movement. TS cars are again of an all open layout and accommodate 84 passengers in the 2+2 and 2+3 mode. Units are gangwayed within sets and have emergency communicating doors in the unit ends. One major break from the PEP prototype has been the forming of trains with two intermediate trailers and the positioning of power equipment under the driving vehicles only, this is provided by eight 110hp GEC 310 traction motors, one mounted on each axle of both motor coaches, power collection being effected by standard third rail pick-up shoes on the outer ends of DMS cars. Standard electro-pneumatic (EP) braking is fitted as well as a dynamic system which is basically rheostatic using power generated during acceleration for braking. Various sophisticated electronic equipment was also fitted to units from new, including a wheel slip/slide protection system, whereby if any trace of wheel slip/slide was monitored by censors fitted to each axle, power would immediately be disconnected if the train was accelerating and not re-applied until the slip/slide indication stopped. If the slip/slide was monitored during braking a decrease in brake pressure was made to the relevant wheel set. Regretfully this system looked all right on the drawing board but when used in reality it proved basically unsatisfactory with trains running by stations and signals because brakes had been released because of only minor wheel slip/slide, and had difficulty in accelerating away from stops on damp and wet rails due to the over sensitivity of the equipment.

Following these problems much development and testing was carried out in this field, especially at the Region's Research and Development section at Strawberry Hill where various modifications have been fitted and tried out on test and service units including the adjustment of brake pressure, of wheel slip/slide tolerance levels and the fitting of wheel scrapers. From late 1982 units were fitted with a WSP (wheel slide protection) button on the driver's desk which if pressed isolated the wheel slip/slide protective system — thus giving the driver overall control of the braking. The Scharfenberg Automatic couplers used on the PEP units were replaced on the production designs by a 'Tightlock' automatic coupling incorporating all physical, electronic and air connections, enabling units to be coupled/uncoupled from the driver's cab.

After units were delivered to the SR, testing was carried out between Strawberry Hill and Shepperton and on the main line between Wimbledon and Basingstoke. As the units were new to the Region driver and staff training had to commence quickly, and during the autumn of 1979 when sufficient units were commissioned to traffic staff training commenced. Most of the training had to be carried out by December 1979 in time for the first revenue earning passenger train on 17 December between Waterloo and Shepperton. By the spring of 1980 the majority of units were on the region and from the commencement of the 1980/81 timetable were scheduled for regular operation between Waterloo, Shepperton, Hampton Court, Chessington and on the Kingston Loop line, gradually taking over a wider area as lines became passed and more units were made available. In connection with R&D testing being carried out at Strawberry Hill Unit No 508.002 was not released to traffic when new and has operated various test programmes not being handed over to the traffic department until December 1982.

Livery applied to units was standard blue/grey from new, with yellow warning end and black centre door. Route indicator (headcode) numbers are not carried, but a destination indicator is provided above the two driving windows. When first introduced units showed the destination above the driver's side window and the intended route above the assistant's window, however this system caused some confusion and the train's starting point is now shown in this position. In November 1981 units Nos 508.042/043 were reformed into three-car sets and hauled to Birkenhead for use on the Merseyrail system followed by sets No 508.039-41 during February 1983. Following the introduction of Class 455 units during early 1983, the remainder of the Class 508 sets will be re-allocated to the LMR at Birkenhead.

178
The delivery of the production 1972 design high-density units commenced on 9 August 1979 when Class 508 No 508.001 arrived on SR tracks hauled by Class 31 No 31.103 from Temple Mills to Strawberry Hill, and is seen here passing Wimbledon. As the unit couplings were not compatible to locomotives a special match wagon, converted from a Conflat, was introduced, having conventional draw gear on one end and tightlock couplings at the other. *John Scrace*

179
Delivery of new units was made to Strawberry Hill, where a commissioning team was stationed. The delivery usually brought ER locomotives to the SR and often a loco would haul new units to Strawberry Hill and return as far as Wimbledon Park with two already commissioned; the locomotive and match wagons then returning to ER. Class 37 No 37.060 hauls units Nos 508.003/004 past New Malden on 27 September 1979 en route to Wimbledon Park from Strawberry Hill. *John Scrace.*

180
After sufficient units were available crew training commenced. For drivers and guards this was normally achieved by running special trains between Waterloo and Shepperton doubling as CM&EE test trips. 17 December 1979 was the first day that fare paying passengers could travel on a Class 508 when the 10.04 Waterloo-Shepperton was formed of units Nos 508.009/008 seen here at Waterloo prior to departure. *Colin Marsden*

181
Units were introduced progressively during early 1980, with a full service from October. Initially the stock could only operate over lines from Waterloo to Hampton Court, Chessington, Shepperton and the Kingston Loop. However this restricted network was enlarged as station platform work was completed. No 508.038 stands at No 2 platform at Waterloo on 24 November 1980 forming a Chessington service. *Steve Montgomery*

182
Class 508s took many months to be fully accepted by the crews and this was not helped by the numerous failures ranging from sticking doors to brake faults. Other problems involved wheel slip, the units were fitted with a complicated wheel slip protection system with brakes on the slipping wheelset being momentarily released. Set No 508.013 whisks up newly fallen snow as it travels between Clapham Junction and Vauxhall with a Hampton Court-Waterloo train on 9 January 1982. *Colin Marsden*

183
Passenger reaction to these new units was mixed, some were well pleased with the design, while others complained bitterly about the seats with a shorter back and narrower width than those on previous units. Other complaints arose from the sliding doors as many passengers thought doors would be automatically opened for them as on the LTE, and on numerous occasions passengers were overcarried. Set No 508.017 departs from Clapham Junction bound for Shepperton on 12 August 1981. *Colin Marsden*

184
The total seating for a four-car Class 508 unit is 320, compared with 404 on a 4SUB, however standing room has been increased enabling up to 280 'strap-hangers' to be accommodated. An eight-car Class 508 formation passes through Clapham Cutting on 17 April 1981 with a Hampton Court-Waterloo service. *Colin Marsden*

185
Many drivers thought that during bad weather the Class 508 fleet would be unable to stand up to the conditions and the automatic wheel slip/slide correction system would render the units nearly immobile, however these fears were unsubstantiated and during some of the worst weather the SR has seen for well over a decade, the fleet kept services going and in fact made better headway than some of the established VEP/CIG style units. Set No 508.023 passes Wimbledon with a Waterloo-Hampton Court service on 11 January 1982. *Colin Marsden*

186
Having tightlock couplings and an electrical/air connection box underneath, the 508 fleet are incompatible with any other SR units, although for emergency assistance purposes any unit or locomotive with a buck-eye coupling can slowly haul a unit, albeit without a through brake connection. The 08.46 Waterloo-Waterloo via Richmond and Kingston approaches Wimbledon on 5 May 1981 led by unit No 508.017. *Colin Marsden*

187
The route between Motspur Park and Effingham Junction was added to the 508 network during 1981, and the lines to Dorking, Horsham and the Hounslow Loop from 1982. No 508.036 accelerates away from Epsom on 5 September 1981 with the 15.12 Waterloo-Effingham Junction service. *Colin Marsden*

188
Surbiton is the farthest south on the main line where the Class 508 fleet operate, this being on the Hampton Court services, although they are permitted to operate as far as Eastleigh for depot and works attention. An eight-car formation takes the 20mph crossing from down slow to down loop line at Surbiton with the 14.56 Waterloo-Hampton Court on 16 April 1981. *Colin Marsden*

189

The coupling together of Class 508 units has caused many problems, when the units are pushed together the covers of the connection box slide open and the electrical and main reservoir connections are made. If for any reason these do not marry up correctly the brakes may not release, or air may escape from the connection, therefore it is necessary for a fitter to be in attendance when units are coupled. An eight-car formation departs from Tolworth led by No 508.032 on 5 May 1981. *Colin Marsden*

190

Although the Class 508 acceleration and de-celeration is far quicker than that of conventional stock, as units are diagrammed to work in conjunction with other stock, no reduction in running times can be made, therefore trains formed of 508 stock sometimes have to wait for time. Departing from Norbiton set No 508.038 works a Shepperton-Waterloo service on 20 March 1981. *Colin Marsden*

191

The South Western Division carry out most maintenance at either Wimbledon, Strawberry Hill or Eastleigh, but work that includes wheelturning and electrical overhauls are dealt with at Selhurst and Slade Green, necessitating special diagrams for units and special crew arrangements. On 6 February 1981 set No 508.016 was captured on film departing from West Croydon on the single line to Wimbledon after receiving attention at Selhurst. *Brian Denton*

192
BR Class 508 No 508.029 was posed alongside Tyne and Wear Metro unit No 4055 and an LTE tunnel cleaning train at Ruislip LT depot on 10 July 1980, as part of an Institute of Engineering Exhibition. The Class 508 was hauled to and from Strawberry Hill between two match wagons by a Class 33 locomotive. *Keith Grafton*

193
Since their introduction during December 1979 only two major mishaps have occurred, a unit was derailed during 1980 on a sand-drag at St Margarets (Twickenham), and on 21 April 1982 the 06.34 Waterloo-Shepperton formed of unit No 508.031 failed to stop at its destination and collided with the buffer stops, ending up hanging precariously over the High Street. This incident was of particular interest to the publishers of this book as their offices are adjacent to the station. *Colin Marsden*

Class 455

The Southern Region purpose built replacement stock for the suburban network was authorised during 1980 and when initially ordered, classification was to be 510 but by the time the stock was delivered in 1982 this was changed to 455. These new generation units were based on the proven Mk III coach design, and incorporated some of the features of the 1972 design high density emu stock. The construction contract was given to BREL York who had previously built the Class 317 sets for the LMR Bedford-St Pancras system, these also being based on the MK III coach design.

The Class 455s stayed in line with SR emu policy of the 1960s by having the power vehicle in the middle of the formation, but as there is no guard's van provided on Class 455s, the vehicle is classified as — MS (Motor Second). Traction power is collected by standard third-rail pick-up shoes carried on the outer ends of the driving cars, and passed to the MS by means of an internal power train line. The formation of each unit is DTS (Driving Trailer Second), MS (Motor Second), TS (Trailer Second), DTS. Externally the vehicles resemble the Class 508s with two sets of double leaf sliding doors on each side, however these are slightly narrower than on the 1972 designed stock. Passenger accommodation is also similar, with low seat backs and plenty of standing room. DTS cars seat 74, while the two intermediate vehicles seat 84 in each. Dynamic braking, a feature of the Class 508, has not been fitted, and braking is provided by an electronically controlled EP system. The coupling of units in multiple has also been changed and the automatic electric connection system under the tightlock coupling featured on 1972 designed stock has been replaced by a non-standard 42 wire control jumper, with nose mounted main reservoir pipes, meaning that the units are not able to operate in multiple with other classes currently in operation on SR. Nose end main reservoir pipes are also carried.

Construction of units commenced late in 1981 at York works, with the first complete sets being despatched to Wolverton for various electrical

194
The first of the new generation purpose built emu stock of Class 455 was delivered to the SR for pre-service inspection on 10 November 1982, being hauled from Wolverton Works where electrical modifications had taken place after construction at York. On 16 November set No 5805 was hauled to Waterloo by Class 33 No 33.018 for a management inspection and is seen here passing Barnes.
Colin Marsden

modifications including the fitting of a wheel-slip over-ride protection system during October 1982. SR Management were anxious to see their new trains and on 10 November 1982 a Waterloo crew was sent with Class 73 No 73.102 light engine to Wolverton to collect unit No 5805, the only unit in suitable condition to be inspected. In line with SR practice units allocated six figure TOPS numbers only carry the last four digits, thus the correct unit number should be 455.805. No 5805 was hauled as an unfitted train at a maximum speed of 40mph to Strawberry Hill where it arrived at 16.00hrs and placed in the CM&EE shed until 16 November when it was hauled to Waterloo for its first inspection. The unit was fitted with its electric pick-up shoes, but was not permitted to operate under its own power, as final testing by GEC was incomplete. After display at Waterloo the unit returned to Strawberry Hill and later Wolverton for completion. Units commenced delivery to the SR for commissioning trials on 20 December 1982 in preparation for driver and staff training. Passenger services utilising Class 455s commenced from the end of March 1983 thus replacing SUB units destined for the breakers yard. Further batches of units based on the Class 455 have now been ordered for use on the Central Division as well as main line services.

195
The Class 455 units commenced passenger operation from the end of March 1983, working on suburban services to and from Waterloo. Set No 5815 heads towards Raynes Park on 14 June 1983 with the 09.15 Horsham-Waterloo service. *Colin J. Marsden*

196
Interior of Class 455 TS vehicle, the car has three seating bays divided by two sets of double leaf sliding doors on each side; as can be seen, the normal seating arrangement is 2+3, however a 2+2 arrangement applies to the seats adjacent to the entrance vestibules. *British Railways*

Departmental Stock

Several units over the years have been passed into departmental or service stock following withdrawal, however the majority of those now in service were rebuilt from stock introduced prior to 1948, and are therefore not covered in this volume but are shown in the companion volume *Southern Electric Multiple-Units 1898-1948*.

Prior to the introduction of the PEP 'new generation' emu trains during the early 1970s the SR operated various trials and tests with equipment on two former LMR 'London District' Class 501 three-car sets. These two units were numbered by the SR 051 and 052 and were introduced during 1969. Being converted from Class 501 sets '162 and '165, all vehicles were renumbered into the departmental numbering sequence thus:

051	052
M61162—DB975027	M61165—DB975030
M70162—DB975028	M70165—DB975031
M75162—DB975029	M75165—DB975032

After their conversion to departmental test vehicles various trials were undertaken mainly involving bogies and traction equipment which was initially fitted to each axle. By late 1970 set 052 was officially withdrawn and set 051 was reformed with various vehicles and equipment from 052, the new 051 formation being: DB975029, DB975027, DB975030. A further short programme of testing was carried out but during 1970 all three cars were stored awaiting disposal at Wimbledon Park. Of the original six cars only two now remain; DB975027 is still fitted with experimental bogies and traction equipment and during 1982 was parked at East Wimbledon depot but was unlikely to undertake any further testing. However car DB975032 was further rebuilt by the SR's CM&EE development section at Strwaberry Hill during 1976 as a mobile test car and fitted with some of the latest electronic equipment. The car was rebuilt to SR emu standards and is now fully operable with them, being fitted with 1963/66 style cab controls, buckeye couplings at both ends and a gangway at the non-driving end. The vehicle undergoes various testing programmes including assisting the recommissioning of the Class 410/411/412 units on return from refurbishment at Swindon Works. Other tests undertaken by the car has involved rail corrugation trials and chopper testing. The livery currently applied is blue/grey and the name *MARS* is allocated but currently not carried.

After finishing their passenger evaluation the three PEP units all passed into departmental service, the two-car set being augmented to three by the addition of a purpose built Trailer Rectifier Car for 25kV ac 750V dc overhead/third rail use and was used on the ER prior to the introduction of Class 313 dual voltage units in 1976. After returning to Derby Railway Technical Centre in 1976 when further test equipment was fitted, the unit was transferred to Scotland to pave the way for the introduction of the Class 314 25kV units. After these trials were completed the set carrying service number 920.001 was parked outside the Railway Technical Centre at Derby where it was still to be seen during 1982. The two four-car sets both went to Derby after withdrawal from the Southern during late 1976 and various trials and tests were undertaken, both sets eventually returning to the SR. From 1978 both were allocated numbers in the departmental series 4001 becoming 056, and 4002 — 057 (although this number has never been carried). 4002 was repainted by the Derby Technical Centre during 1979 in advanced passenger train livery of black, red and grey but retaining its yellow ends. Set 056 remained in all blue and after being dumped at Strawberry Hill and Wimbledon was removed during 1981 back to Derby, where it still lays awaiting a decision on its future. In 1981 set 4002 operated a series of trial runs on the SR involving bogie and traction equipment, normally between Wimbledon and Basingstoke, and for this testing, the bogies throughout the set were replaced and the unit was equipped with modified power bogies to the driving vehicles only, the former MSO intermediate vehicles being carried on a newly designed trailer bogie. At the present time 4002 is dumped at Clapham Junction with a very uncertain future.

In 1981 two standard Mk 1 loco-hauled coaches joined the ranks of the SR departmental fleet when they became 'Romeo' and 'Juliet' and allocated running numbers DB975808/809 respectively. These two vehicles were fitted with chopper train control equipment, one car containing a system manufactured by Brush and the other by GEC. Major external rebuilding of the coaches took place including the fitting of powered bogies, third-rail pick-up shoes, high level air,

power and control jumpers. Trial running of these cars is usually confined to the Shepperton branch mostly at night and carried out with two of three former 2HAP (Class 414) units which were taken into departmental stock during 1982.

From May 1982 when a substantial number of 2HAP units were withdrawn three units Nos 6086, 6121 and 6142 were transferred to the Research and Development section at Strawberry Hill and renumbered 051-053 respectively. At the time of going to press it is understood that these units will only act as traction power for various test trains and are unlikely to be converted in any way.

197
Although de-icing units formed of former SR stock are covered in Volume I, this view of set No 001 has been included here because when converted in 1967 it operated with one coach of 2EPB No 5750, as the correct vehicle was not ready for introduction; the EPB coach only acted as a tractor and carried no de-icing equipment. During 1969 the correct car for 001 was completed and car No S65364 of unit 5750 returned to passenger carrying use. 001 is seen here at Shepperton. *Ian Allan Library*

198
The former SR units converted to de-icing trains became life expired during the late 1970s and a further fleet of units were authorised, being converted from redundant SUB motor coaches and converted to their new use at Selhurst. During the rebuilding work cars were rebuilt from the frames upwards and modern cabs comparable to EPB/VEP units were installed. Each of the major depots on the Region has an allocation of de-icing units which operate over most of their routes each night during winter months. Set No 008 is shown here at Wimbledon Park, its home depot.
Colin Marsden

199
After the completion of the passenger carrying test programme the two four-car PEP units were passed into departmental use, operating a number of test trains, mainly involving the development of bogie and traction equipment. Set No 4002 visited Derby during 1979/80 and returned to the SR painted in Inter-City *APT* colours. Departing from Wimbledon Park station set No 4002 works a bogie test train to Basingstoke on 9 May 1980. *Colin Marsden*

200

The original 2PEP No 2001 which was taken into departmental use during the mid-1970s and numbered 920.001, operated on both Eastern and Scottish regions before being stored at the Derby Railway Technical Centre. Here No 920.001 and PEP No 4002 are seen side by side outside the RTC during 1979. Note the additional air pipe on the front of 920.001. *Colin Marsden*

201

For bogie and traction motor tests, two former Class 501 three-car sets were transferred to departmental use on the SR during 1969. Some tests were carried out but the cars saw little use after 1972 and were placed in store around the system for several years. DB975029 shown here painted in early blue livery with small yellow warning panel, stands in sidings at Twickenham on 5 March 1980. *Colin Marsden*

RMB Cars S1872 and S1873

If special trains were operated formed of TC or other emu stock not fitted with a buffet car and catering facilities were required, difficulties arose, so two of the Region's RMB (Restaurant Miniature Buffet) cars were fitted with emu style end connections enabling them to be formed in standard emu train formations. The equipment fitted to the RMBs was high level air pipes and a 27 wire control jumper receptacle.

The two vehicles were withdrawn from capital stock at the end of 1982 and stored. From May 1983 the vehicles were reinstated and used marshalled between a 3 and 4CIG to form two temporary 8MIG units, due to a shortage of buffet units for Waterloo-Portsmouth services.

202
SR allocated RMBs Nos S1872/3 are not officially emu vehicles but have been included in this book as they are fitted with 27 wire control jumper equipment and high level air pipes, enabling them to operate within emu formations. Normally these cars are used between TC units to provide buffet facilities for special or railtour trains. S1872 is shown here between two TCs at Addiscombe whilst working an enthusiasts special on 20 January 1979. *Brian Morrison*

Southern Region General Manager's Saloon

The SR's General Manager's saloon is not officially an emu but as it can operate fully with most emu formations it has been included in this volume. The coach was converted from a 6B buffet car No S60755 during 1969 and when rebuilding work was carried out the internal layout was redesigned with a small centre guard's compartment and two observation saloons, one at each end of the car, both with full width end windows. A driving position is provided at both ends. When converted the saloon was fitted with necessary equipment to enable it to operate in multiple with modern emu stock (except Classes 455/508 and 4SUB units), as well as push-pull fitted Class 33 and 73 locomotives. On the car's nose end are standard emu connections together with a train heating cable on the buffer beam. A two position headcode is fitted under the centre window with three spotlights at cant rail height. Shoe gear is fitted to the underframe to enable the vehicle to pick up its own supply for heating and lighting if required. Between the bogies a set of air operated retractable steps are provided for lineside inspections. The livery applied is blue/grey, and the car is always kept at Stewarts Lane.

On 29 July 1981 the saloon hit world wide fame when it was used to convey The Prince and Princess of Wales from Waterloo to Romsey on the first stage of their honeymoon. The vehicle was again the subject of much press coverage during May 1982 when it conveyed Pope John Paul II from Gatwick Airport to Victoria on the first stage of his British tour.

203
Another vehicle not officially classed as an emu is the Southern Region's General Manager's Saloon, converted from a Hastings line buffet car in March 1969. This vehicle is not fully compatible with modern emus, Class 33/1 and 73 locomotives and is fitted with emu driving positions at each end. The vehicle is numbered TDB975025 and is usually kept at Stewarts Lane. *Colin Marsden*

Construction Data

Type	*Original Numbering*	*Re-numbering*	*Year Introduced*	*Formation*	*Notes*
4EPB	5001-5053	415.xxx-415.xxx*	1951-1954	MBSO-TS-TS-MBSO	*Renumbered out of sequence when passing through works. 415.401 series.
4EPB	5101-5260	415.xxx-415.xxx*	1953-1957	MBSO-TS-TS-MBSO	
4EPB	5261-5264	415.xxx-415.xxx*	1960-1979	MBSO-TS-TS-MBSO	Formed from spare cars
4EPB	5301-5370	415.301-415.370	1960-1963	MBSO-TS-TS-MBSO	Facelifted units will be renumbered in the 415.6xx range.
2EPB	5651-5684	416.651-416.684	1959	MBSO-DTS	
2EPB	5701-5779	416.701-416.779	1953-1958	MBSO-DTS	
2EPB	5781-5795	416.681-416.695	1954-1955	MBSO-DTS	Introduced 1954/5 for NER transferred to SR in 1963
2EPB	5800	—	1960	MBSO-DTS	
4EPB	5401-54xx	415.401-415.4xx	1979-	MBSO-TS-TS-MBSO	Facelifted Class 415 (4EPB) units
2EPB	6301-63xx	416.301-416.3xx	1982-	MBSO-DTS	Facelifted Class 416 (2EPB) units
4CEP	7101-7104	411.5xx-411.5xx*	1956-1957	MBSO-TSK-TCK-MBSO	*Renumbered out of sequence when passing through works
4CEP	7105-7211	411.5xx-411.6xx*	1958-1963	MBSO-TSK-TCK-MBSO	
4BEP	7001-7002	411.5xx-411.5xx*	1956-1957	MBSO-TCK-TRB-MBSO	
4BEP	7003-7012	411.5xx	1959-1961	MBSO-TCK-TRB-MBSO	
4BEP	7013-7022	412.301-412.310	1982	DMS-TBC-TRB-DMS	Refurbished Class 411 stock
4BEP	7153	411.301	1979	DMS-TBC-TS-DMS	Prototype refurbished unit
4CEP	1501-1620	—	1979-1983	DMS-TBC-TS-DMS	Refurbished 4CEP/BEP units
2HAP	6001-6173	414.001-414.173	1957-1963	MBSO-DTC	
2HAP	5601-5636	418.604-418.636	1958-1959	MBSO-DTC	Now 2SAP units many now withdrawn and converted to Class 415
MLV	68001-68010	—	1959-1961	MLV	
TLV	68201-68206	—	1968	TLV	Converted from BG. Now back to the loco-hauled fleet
4CIG	7301-7336	421.701-421.736	1964-1966	DTC-TS-MBSO-DTC	
4CIG	7337-7438	421.737-421.738	1970-1973	DTC-TS-MBSO-DTC	
4BIG	7031-7048	422.101-422.118	1965-1966	DTC-TRB-MBSO-DTC	To be reclassified 422 from 420 during 1983
4BIG	7049-7058	422.201-422.210	1970	DTC-TRB-MBSO-DTC	
3TC	301-303	—	1966	DTS-TBS-DTS	Now converted to 4TC units

Type	*Original Numbering*	*Re-numbering*	*Year Introduced*	*Formation*	*Notes*
4TC	401-428	491.401-491.428	1966-1967	DTS-TBS-TFK-DTS	
4TC	429-434	491.429-491.434	1974	DTS-TBS-TFK-DTS	429-431 converted from 3TC above
4REP	3001-3011	432.001-432.011	1967	DMS-TBF-TRB-DMS	To be reclassified 432 from 430 during 1983
4REP	3012-3015	432.012-432-015	1974	DMS-TBF-TRB-DMS	
4VEC	041-046	485.041-485.046	1967	MBSO-TSO-DTS-MBSO	Converted from LTE stock
3TIS	031-036	486.031-486.036	1967	MBSO-TSO-MBSO	Converted from LTE stock
4VEP	7701-7894	423.701-423.894	1967-1973	DTC-TSO-MBSO-DTC	
8VAB	8001	—	1968	DTC-MBSO-DTC-DTC-MBSO-TRB-MBSO-DTC	Converted from VEP stock
4VEG	7901-7912	427.901-427.912	1978-1979	DTC-TSO-MBSO-DTC	Converted from VEP stock
4PEP	4001-4002	056-057	1971	MBSO-MSO-MSO-MBSO	Now in departmental service
2PEP	2001	920.001	1972	MBSO-MBSO	Now in departmental service
4-508	—	508.001-508.043	1979-1980	MBSO-TSO-TSO-MBSO	Some units now operating on LMR
4CAP	—	413.201-413.212	1982	DTC-MBSO-MBSO-DTC	Formed of two 2HAP units for Coastway use.
4CAP	—	413.301-413.311	1982	DTC-MBSO-MBSO-DTC	
2SAP	(5939) 6039	414.939	1982	DTS-MBSO	Converted from 2HAP unit
4-455	—	455.801-455.874	1982	DTS-MS-TS-DTS	
RB	S1758-S1759	—	1968	RB	Loco-hauled Buffet car fitted with through electrical and high level air pipes for emu operation